Glenn Martin (1950 -) grew up in Sydney, Australia. He lived in the hills on the far north coast of New South Wales for twenty years before coming back to Sydney. He is a writer on management, training and business ethics. He has been a manager of organisations in the community sector, a high school teacher, psychiatric nurse, community worker, social researcher, tutor in business ethics, and editor of professional publications. His other books include:

> *Human Values and Ethics in the Workplace*
> *The Little Book of Ethics*
> *The Ten Thousand Things: A story of the lived*
>   *experience of the I Ching*
> *Sustenance*

See Glenn's website at www.glennmartin.com.au

To the bush and back to business

Glenn Martin

To the bush and back to business
By Glenn Martin

Published 2012 by G.P. Martin Publishing
Websites: www.glennmartin.com.au
              www.ethics.andvalues.com.au
Contact: info@glennmartin.com.au

National Library of Australia
Cataloguing-in-Publication entry
Author: Martin, Glenn.
Title: To the bush and back to business / Glenn Martin.
ISBN: 978 0 9804045 5 5 (pbk.)
Subjects: Martin, Glenn.
Dewey Number: A828.409

Book layout, design and photos by the author
Typeset in Bookman Old Style 11 pt
Printed by Lulu.com

Author's Foreword

I know authors don't have to do this, and maybe some readers would prefer I didn't. Who wants to read an author's foreword? Just get on with the story. Well, there's the issue of precedent for a start. I wrote an author's foreword for *The Ten Thousand Things* and for *Sustenance*. A precedent has been set.

And besides, when you read the book you might wonder how it was written. It was in fact written under the same constraint as the two books mentioned, that is, as a project to write a book of at least 50,000 words in one month – National Novel Writing Month, or NanoWrimo. That requirement does to writers what they generally have a strong wish to avoid – it demands that they perform on the spot. With this goal and time frame, there is no time for second thoughts or regrets; you wrote what you wrote today and now you have to figure out what to say next. And don't think about it for too long. The only option is to keep going, and I did, day upon day.

The book was a surprise to me. In my two earlier books, a definite story announced itself to me quite early on: I knew that that was the story I had to tell. This time, a "neat", "historical" event did not appear; I just had to keep digging. It was the theme that took centre stage. I realised after a while that I was writing about why I left the city as a young man – what drove me, and what eventuated.

Is this book a memoir? At one point within, I reject the idea, and I stand by my reasons. But then, when I applied for an ISBN, I had to nominate a category, and I had to relent. It seemed to be the closest fitting category. Hence, you will see that the subject of the book is "Martin, Glenn". But that is not so. I am just the vehicle.

The story is the thing, and I haven't told this story before. It is when I have to write that I think most deeply. Writing it forced me to grapple with things that had just sat comfortably (or uncomfortably) below the surface for a long time.

I hadn't planned to take an archaeological approach. That happened because in writing about the time when I left the city, phrases of poems I had written at that time started to come back to me, and I remembered that I had a whole boxful of these poems and stories. Of course, taking the lid off the box was a matter of some trepidation. It might all be stomach-churning rubbish, all angst and naivety. And I worried about including poetry in a prose book; I think it's generally problematic to try and put those two kinds of sensibilities together.

But I feel that I have accommodated myself appropriately. I think the stories and poems belong here. I'm not claiming greatness for them, but nor am I apologising for them. They are voices that were part of my journey, they are expressions of how it was at certain points along the way. And I don't keep journals, so I wasn't striving for historical (place, time, people) accuracy. In a way I'm glad. The poems and stories are truer.

I came back to the city, as the book title indicates, and here I am, in some kind of relationship to the business world. The core of the book for me, that came as a realisation when I had finished writing, was that there is a continuity and cohesiveness about my life that I (almost) didn't expect. In some ways I was thinking that I had started in one place, and gone here and there, and happened to come back to the same city, but there was really little to tie it together except loss and failure.

Well, there is indeed loss and failure, but my ideals and passions seem (to me) remarkably persistent and resilient. I trust you will see it too. Enjoy.

Glenn Martin
Sydney, May 2012

1

I have come to a stop. And things have conspired to make me stop. Jobs have been coming my way with less frequency, and there is no longer anyone living with me. In fact, I worked out last night that this is the first time I have been living alone in over twenty years. It is not alarming, it is not fearful, it is not empty. I have a feeling of spaciousness. I remind myself at times during the day. Spaciousness.

Of course there are still obligations. There are still some jobs to do, there is still maintenance, there are still minor interests. There is still noise. But in this new space things are slower, and I wonder about my ambitions. I would not have thought of myself as a person who harboured ambitions, and yet I think there are such boats in my harbour. And if so, I have not been greatly successful. I have had no great career, I have not accumulated honours, fame or funds. I do not even have a cohort of professional friends, for I have moved from industry to industry. Instead of peaking, I seem to have petered out.

And I baulk at saying even this, because it veers in the direction of self-pity, which is a ferocious monster that can devour a person. It is a Wang demon whose blood runs black and who sucks you into the ground. I know there is no need to be too disparaging of my past; there are many respectable achievements strewn around in it, things done well, some victories. It's just that it all falls away, and here I am still.

I have been told to enjoy myself. To remember that. I've earned it (they say). And a friend sent me a quote the other day, from the poet, Rumi: "You have woken up late, lost and perplexed. But don't rush to your books looking for knowledge. Pick up the flute instead and let your heart play." I agree. I usually do agree with Rumi. But I would contend that I do enjoy the things I do. It's just that some of the things I do would not look like enjoyment to other people.

I've just spent a week of long days and long nights writing a paper on ethics. It was 20,000 words and involved a lot of research – immersion in dozens of writers' thoughts and works, as well as dredging up memories of books I've read over a span of forty years. You have to follow the thread of a thought, and then things pop up. So it happened that, near the end, it was appropriate to call upon Theodore Roszak, from a book published in 1972 called *The Making of a Counter Culture*. I found the book on my shelves with remarkable rapidity, and the passage I wanted, with a bookmark at the page and the exact words I wanted highlighted.

I'm just saying, satisfaction is a personal thing. King Wen says that sometimes you should be satisfied to stay at home, to stay within your court with the gate firmly closed. Do not scatter yourself about in idle chatter with this one and that one, agitated. Do not strive to be prominent. At one point he says the flying bird came and left him a message, and the message was, it is not appropriate for you to soar. Remember the little; that makes you sincere and trustworthy.

I think, is this all a bit "quietist"? Are our lives meant to be menial? Should I forego any vestige of wanting? But I recall, there was a visit recently, so unusual that I took a photo of it. It was a visit by four birds. Not one, but four. Four black cockatoos with red tails came and sat in my favourite tree in my yard. Right here in the suburbs. They made their raucous sound as they flew in – that's how you know you are

2

getting a visit. I came out to see if it was really black cockatoos. They used to come to where I lived before, in the country, in a forested valley near a creek. They would come when the weather was on the turn, and rain was on the way. They would fly in great arcs about the trees, in small groups, and land near the house, a great circus of noise, town criers screeching, "Wake up, wake up. Sumptuous weather approaching."

When the black cockatoos sat in my favourite tree, they paused. The message was just the silence, as if to say: it's okay to stop. Indeed, necessary, if you like. I wasn't quite sure what the message was at the time. Black cockatoos are so striking that you always think there is great portent in their appearance. But for some mornings after that I sat just outside the door of my study for a while, with my cup of hot green tea, and looked at the sky. You could say it was "open eyes meditation". If you like.

What do I get from sky? This: for all my activity, desire and restlessness, it remains blue and deep. It has its own restless spirit too, as clouds come and go, but it is able to accommodate them. The sky is the great house that accommodates whatever comes. I enjoy clouds, but I love the constancy of sky.

So I deal with small affairs, content. Frugality is better than excess. After bliss there are cups of tea, and indeed, abundance.

2

Outside the gate, business goes on. They say it is a world where good people do bad things. But supposing this were the case, I don't see any general spirit of willingness to look into this unfortunate state of affairs. Who is asking, how can we get these supposedly good people to actually do good things? It always seems rather late when we recognise that something is a bad thing. Up until then we keep thinking the thing is good, or at least acceptable, or widespread, or inevitable. We keep lurching towards our unseemly ends.

I say, if you take something to its logical conclusion you've taken it too far. That's the trouble with logic. So here we are, in this society full of stuff, and of course it's fun, but have we become attached to the race, and don't know how to stop? How many clothes are enough? How big does your house need to be? How often do you need to replace your kitchen or your car?

There is a madness about all this. We have created this pattern over a period of two hundred years, and asked Adam Smith to bless it. Produce, buy, consume, replace, ad infinitum. Although, it now appears, there may not be an ad infinitum. This whole pattern is unsustainable, but we don't know what a sustainable world would look like, economically, socially or, most importantly, in terms of lifestyle. That's why I ended up in the bush forty years ago. There were a number of people who precipitated that recourse, and Theodore Roszak was one of them.

It's difficult to know what is best. One avenue is to be political, to join political groups and be vocal, to demand change. And sometimes it works. When I was about twenty I joined in the Moratorium marches to end Australia's involvement in the war in Vietnam. I was among hundreds of thousands of others in cities around Australia. I sat in the middle of the road in George Street in Sydney listening to speeches from the steps of the Town Hall. This was unprecedented. Nothing like this had happened in my life. People prevailing over traffic for a start.

It got unpleasant. When the huge throng set off to march down the street, squadrons of police set upon us. They were doing their job, trying to stop a mob of people from walking down the street. (After all, there was traffic to consider.) Many of the police were prepared to be violent in seeking to fulfil their objective. This was also unprecedented in my experience. But in retrospect, why would it have been otherwise? The police are instructed to maintain what is normally understood as "order" and they are trained in methods for ensuring that objective. If the occasion seems to require truncheons, when people prove to be contrary, then truncheons become the order of the day.

Nevertheless, the Moratoriums worked. The troops came home. The government changed its mind. Which is to say, it had probably already realised that the demon they had gone to fight, the Domino theory of Communism (if one country in Asia falls to Communism then the others will all follow) was not true, so in fact there was nothing to be lost by bringing the troops home. But any greater cause was lost. If I had thought this episode would precipitate a change in society towards a way of governance and a form of lifestyle that were more in harmony with the earth, I was certainly wrong.

There was much talk of working within the system to change it. But I had read Herbert Marcuse, and I figured he was right. The ruling group (sorry, it's not that simple, the concept of the "ruling group", or hegemony, is more rigid than the reality, but let's not make it too complicated for ourselves) knows that the best way to eradicate opposition is to absorb it into itself. And some of the leaders of the protest movement seemed only too willing to pursue the cause by "working from within". Soon after, it looked more like a fast track to the top in the ruling group for them. With a haircut, a new suit, and a freshly groomed belief system.

It was around this time that John Lennon sang, "You say you want a revolution, yeah? You better free your mind instead." The answer for me was to leave. It was the violence that had affected me more than anything else. Passionate violence I can understand – people get angry and end up hitting each other. In a small group of people where there is little power and not much in the way of material goods at stake, friends pull the two fighters apart and tell them to cool down and make up.

What I saw in the police action was calculated method, the intent, at the least, to stop people from doing something even if it meant smashing heads and breaking bones. And for some, it was more than that: it was the enjoyment of the opportunity, the licence to hurt people with impunity. Especially when they feared what the people might stand for – a threat of some unnamed kind.

Of course, many among the protesters were jubilant about what they stood for. It was freedom. I, on the other hand, thought that while freedom is fundamental to living well, it is an empty concept until you quantify what you mean by it. And many of the biggest cheerleaders for "freedom" seemed remarkably reticent to take this next step.

Politics, the great hope for social change, soured very quickly for me. The surge that came soon after the Moratoriums, with the election of the Labor Party after 23 years "in the wilderness", and the ascension of Gough Whitlam to Prime Minister, was but a brief, although important, flutter. I stood in the queue to vote in the election after Gough Whitlam was, in unprecedented fashion, sacked by the Governor-General after a mere three years in government, and felt the collective determination in the voters around me to put the lid back on the bottle, to never let the genie out again. And so it happened. Well, Whitlam lost the election, and the genie had to go elsewhere.

3

I have said "unprecedented" several times. Is that sensationalism, a vanity? I think not. It was such a time. In the great sweep of things, of course, things move more slowly, but consider: recently, a radio station gathered votes to produce a list of the top twenty songs of the last fifty years, and John Lennon's "Imagine" was at the top of the list. Number one. Imagine that. It was at this time of tumultuousness that John Lennon gave us a psalm for our times, a song that could fill all our eyes with tears together and make our hearts burst with love, again and again. Every time. At least now, some of us knew what we were looking for, and for those who did not understand or did not wish to, it yet served to calm the spirit.

In ancient times, King Wen built a magic tower, from where to observe the omens of the spirit. He watched the skies from his ritual platform raised high above the ground, watching for the appearance of the Mandated Star that would confirm the commands of Heaven to be implemented in the world below. He read the omens of the spirit that appeared in the world around him and penetrated deeply into their meaning, to seize the influx of the hidden energies. He drank dark wine out of the sacred bronze vessel and called the spirits to be present.

In my time, the manifestations were more confusing. Christo came to Sydney with acres of nylon fabric and wrapped up an entire landscape, a headland on the harbour. It became a great event, with mystery, amusement and awe. He was inundated with volunteers who had heard of his great public wrappings overseas. They spent days spreading fabric and tying it down, like a big present or a big secret. But I never quite understood, and I was even less sure that others understood what it all meant. It seemed to work because it was, shall we say, unprecedented? Christo went onto further ventures in the world, in later years wrapping buildings (the Pont Neuf in Paris, the Reichstag in Berlin), miles of fencing in farmland in California, and islands in Biscayne Bay in Miami (in pink).

I was quiet for months after the ugly street scenes in the Moratorium. That urge to pen and broadcast a manifesto was stilled. Months later, the resolve crystallised, to avoid the joining of crowds. I thought, "No good can come of that." I thought, "Do not plead sanity. Only the mad are free." They were like stones dropping out of my pocket and rolling to the ground. I watched those thoughts, separate from me, smooth, heavy, rock-hard, feeling their weight but also knowing I was not them.

I saw that there were those who turned their anger into hatred. There were underground groups who met and railed against the establishment. They argued political philosophy and produced angry street posters, all rendered in reds and blacks. They festooned small suburbs with what nowadays we would call a brand. At the time it was taken to be misguided passion. For me, it was just too much commitment to maintaining a mood that was not constructive. Focusing, certainly, but incapable of knowing what to do if they ever "won".

I turned to reading. I wended my way along a self-chosen path, one writer opening up a new vista and then another writer coming along to fill out some other aspect of the terrain. Like King Wen, I was watching the lands and charting the skies. I read Dietrich Bonhoeffer, Jacques Ellul, C.H. Dodd, and treasured what I learnt. I wrote poems, striving to articulate the unvoiced thoughts and feelings within. Years later, in a personal development course, we were asked who our heroes had been when we were growing up. I couldn't answer, because I couldn't think of any people I knew who had functioned for me in that way. Perhaps occasionally, perhaps in a limited way, some people had, but none that I would have called heroes.

Now, I have no hesitation. My heroes were among these writers that I read so voraciously. In fact, I have a book about Bonhoeffer that has the series title, "Heroes of the faith". One thing that Bonhoeffer did for me was to put the concept of freedom into context. Towards the end of his life, confined in a Nazi jail (gaol) and interrogated daily for months on end, he wrote a poem that had four stanzas, headed "Discipline", "Action", "Suffering" and "Death". Here he articulated for me that freedom was associated with discipline: "If you set out to seek freedom, then learn above all, discipline of soul and senses".

He taught me that your life should reflect what you assert, and that after you have determined what you think about something, you must act – "The world of thought is an escape; freedom comes only through action". But that sometimes there is no scope for action at all, and then you must realise that this is the case: "Powerless, alone, you see the end of your action. Still, you take a deep breath and lay your struggle for justice, quietly and in faith, into a mightier hand." Bonhoeffer was killed by his captors not long before the end of the Second World War.

And from C.H. Dodd I learned a simple message, about authority. He was a Roman Catholic theologian who was bold enough to ask the question, "What is the authority for this proposition?" I learned from him to ask that question everywhere I went. It was amazing how that question dissolved walls, empires, bullies and idiots. It is a question that pushes you into new territories. You discover that a great show of grandeur or pomposity can rest on the most dubious of foundations, and then the world can change.

Jacques Ellul was another wonder. What I found remarkable was that no one in school, my church or my university had told me about him, and when I mentioned him, no one even seemed to have heard of him. But his extraordinary mind, and life, revolutionised my thinking. He was both a theologian (unusually, a French evangelical Christian) and a sociologist, and for a time in the 1940s he had been the mayor of Bordeaux. He had two streams of work, one sociological and the other Christian. He provided me with in-depth analyses of major aspects of life – violence, propaganda and what for me was his tour de force: *The Technological Society.*

Written in 1954, it transformed my understanding of how society works. Apparently, for many people, Ellul's book on "the technological society" was a mere diatribe against modern technology. But that altogether misconceives what he says. His thought is far deeper and more pervasive than that. What he is really attacking is the idea of technique, when it is applied to every aspect of our life. And he is not even attacking technique as such; he is attacking the idea that the search for efficiency is becoming the most important thing in our lives; it is becoming the end purpose, it usurps the place of human purpose, when it ought only to be the means, the servant, and subsidiary to the real stuff of human life.

I think this is what Aboriginal people see when they look from their traditional context at white man's culture; they see a lot of technique and they wonder how it serves the purpose of living, which is to live as part of the Great Mother, earth.

I wrote a poem that was a brief history of man (as it was in those days before we realised we had excluded women). There were three stages:

> You stoop with your eyes to the stars,
> carve out songs in the hollow silence,
> bend back, work, sweat, fear and love,
> and at the end of the day
> are collected into Abraham's bosom.

> You segregate the world in rows of test-tubes,
> write an equation for the universe,
> observe, analyse, classify, hypothesise,
> and live forever as the man who discovered atoms.

> You strive for your seat in the train,
> spin your own plastic cocoon,
> pay bills, press buttons, obey rules, advance,
> and hand your passport to
> the automatically forgiving, computerised God.

And there was a final, ironic line: "Press Button B if no one answers". That wouldn't make sense today, but when I wrote it, in public telephones, you inserted your four pennies into a slot and then dialled the number. If someone answered you pressed Button A to allow the pennies to be taken into the machine; if no one answered, you pressed Button B to get your pennies back.

How efficient we have become. Now all the pennies happen behind the scenes; we just touch the screen to dial, and there are no visible strings or wires attached. Yet the question of human purpose has no better answers in society now than it did then. The only clue is that people still get tears in their eyes when they hear that John Lennon song..... "Imagine.....It's easy if you try".

11

4

I am still sitting in my study. No one is stopping me. Rain has started, and the tyres of the cars on the road outside sound different, flicking up fine water as they pass. The other sound is the softness of raindrops meeting the leaves of the trees, a great, gentle multitude that is received gratefully and gathered in. This is how life continues. I do nothing to make it continue, I simply observe that it is happening, and that is how it is.

Yes, it's hard to do this (nothing). I read a passage from Bonhoeffer again, a poem he wrote during his imprisonment. He asks, "Who am I?" and he thinks that other people see him as calm and strong, a man of faith in the midst of monstrous circumstances. But from the inside, he is aware of his anger, his restlessness, his tiredness, his sadness. And yet he was a man of faith. He was able to contain all of that seething and fear and bring it to tameness within his larger vision. It was a continual experience and quest, to abide in that larger vision.

So this is what I was reading while my own world was falling apart, while I was becoming disenchanted with the social institutions of my day. The outcry over the Vietnam War was not really about that. None of us understood what was happening in Vietnam. I'd read a little bit about the history – the French colonialists, the unrest and uprisings following the Second World War, the Communist movement, the rise of Ho Chi Minh – but it was sketchy and unreal. And most people had not read anything at all. So the anti-war movement and the mass protests were not about any political

12

judgement relating to the military actions in Vietnam. It was discontent about what was happening in our own society.

I think that, for the most part, such movements are only dimly aware of the real sources of discontent. They are a trigger for all sorts of feelings to surface. In Australia, much of it was about our identity as an independent nation, about breaking our subservience to England and the United States. But, even from this point in time, I can't think of any better explanation. It seemed to be primarily a catalyst, whose purpose was to break up the monolithic, moribund society we had become.

So many things happened in society in the lead-up to the Moratoriums. Pop music happened and became the vehicle for great shifts in social attitudes. After the Moratoriums there were big shifts in many areas of society. The brief Gough Whitlam years saw the eventuation of many liberating changes. There were, for example, the first moves towards recognising the existence of Aborigines respectfully.

But I was not assuaged by any of this. My discontent persisted. It was more fundamental than what could be addressed satisfactorily by the abolition of the Privy Council as the court of final legal appeal, or the regionalisation of Australia, or better cities. It was Jacques Ellul's ideas that had got under my skin. With the best of intentions of the new breed of politicians, it seemed to me, the best we would end up with would still just be "progress".

When I read Theodore Roszak, it reinforced what Ellul had been saying. Roszak's book starts with a chapter denouncing the technocratic society. It is lively stuff. Of education, as an example of how our society operates, he says we call it "'the life of the mind', the 'pursuit of truth'. But it is a matter of machine-tooling the young to the needs of our various baroque bureaucracies: corporate, governmental, military, trade union, educational."

This is what I had zoned in on – the idea of society turned into a mindless machine that has forgotten what its purpose is. A society that only knows how to perpetuate itself in its external manifestations – structures, processes and roles. And even this would not have been so bad except for a small voice that kept whispering to me, "This is all there is. This is all there is."

I wrote poems regularly during this time. There was one about nature as an ageing woman, vigour lost, surpassed by a brash and unattractive technological world:

The earth mother lays out her dress again,
surprising the afternoon sun,
but stiffer, and trying to remember the truth,
lying like a lost broach
among the age-creased flowers.
Sun in the dry cracks;
the boys no longer come.
In a storm of purpose they would strip
the branches for whips.

Now they sit in pressed shirts
on the verandah,
awash in the heat and their beer slops.

The earth mother retches
in stale, pot-plant colours, odours,
clears her coarse throat
in the rectilinear shade
of an aluminium easy chair:
the ascendant truth.

What was missing, even from Roszak, was a recognition of the looming catastrophe for the sustainability of humans on the planet. Scientists were

14

already beginning to report on it. The Club of Rome's report on a comprehensive suite of ecological problems, from population growth to food supply, oil supply and pollution, made the front cover of *Time* magazine in 1972. But everyone was busy discussing social reforms and enjoying new freedoms. Cars were still getting bigger, houses were becoming better appointed with appliances.

It's no fun talking about doom. It was just too big a concept to capture news media or politicians. The scientists were treated like Chicken Little, who thought the sky would fall on his head. The idea that all of this progress might somehow be wrong, or ill-advised, was almost blasphemy. I remember a short verse I made up, which I thought summed up the prevailing stance, a belligerent and arrogant interpretation of Christianity:

Poor Chicken Little,
thought the sky would fall on his head;
poorer scientist,
knows there is none (to dread).

It was saying that the scientists knew nothing important, because they were godless, in the arid sense of that word. I gave up. I decided to leave, and create another life, quietly and far from the city.

5

I am not a good historian. I don't keep notes, and I'm not good at remembering dates or details. I have vague recollections and key moments. I have memories of feelings. I have feelings in retrospect about those past times. And I have a sporadic collection of poems from across all of the years. That's the best I can do.

And I must say, here, that this is no memoir. It is a story, that's all. I read a statement about memoirs. The writer said, "A memoir is, perhaps, the last thing one needs in life, somewhat like a coffin." I agree. Memoir is to me like the last word before one dies. As yet, I have no interest in dying, I am still in the midst of whatever it is that is happening; it is not ready to be wrapped and folded and consigned to a museum. These pasts are still volatile.

I set out to recover a sense of peace and possibility. Perhaps if I found it for myself and a small community, this would be significant for the society I was leaving, and if not, then at least it would be good in itself. Not that I ever wanted to preach; I just wanted to be able to say, yes, there is a way.

I left my attempts at academia. Philosophy, psychology, education, as they were practised, all could be summed up adequately by what I'd read in the likes of Roszak, Marcuse and McLuhan. I started reading *Earth Garden* and *The Last Whole Earth Catalogue*. I found I was reaching regularly into the part of my brain that prefers to express things in poetry. I make no claims about the "quality" of my poems. I concluded that the attitudes of poetry magazines were, shall I say, idiosyncratic and arbitrary? And I would also say, to be truthful, I don't think I have much interest in poems as a literary form if that means the poems are extracted from context.

I write poems when I want to express something about the situation I am in, when I am trying to make sense of something and prose doesn't seem to be the appropriate vehicle to express it because the meaning lies deep inside a feeling, not in a logical pattern of thought. So taking the poem away from the context seems dangerous and misguided, at the least. Or self-defeating. (Oh, yes, I know there is the stuff of argument in this, but let's just let it stand this way for now.)

I was leading up to this poem:

On the side of the lowly

One by one the heroes have all died;
they grace the heavens with their wisdom in retrospect.
Here we carve out days upon days,
seldom seeming to make a difference.

We have powers enormous at our fingertips,
words stream out of our mouths like rivers of sand.
The underside of all this is patently manifest:
more words, less meaning,
more power, less purpose.

Yet we continue as if it were not so,
as if an emperor still sat on an emperor's throne
and dispensed ample portions of mercy and justice,
and honoured the love of beauty.
I go down, separate, to where I can hear again,
the call of dumb creatures, bird and tree and stone,
I have to bring myself back and start again.

I have built a memorial tablet to the ancestors;
in fact I have built rather a lot.
Some of them are only small,
while others are more elaborate.
I trace the paths that they trod
and I forgive them their sins,
for they have learned now
while we have yet to learn.
I honour the ones who have gone
as I go forward
to grace action with honest intent,
to wrest honour from lords of deceit,
to bear light into prisons of defeat.
The meaning is closer now,

17

like thunder in the mountains,
like rain on the face.
Om Om Om

Obscure enough, even in context? Ah well, poets
do what they can, I suppose. It's hard work
summoning meaning out of darkness. I give away
several things in this poem. I tell you that my mission
now is to reconnect with the earth, with the natural
world. I tell you that I have taken on the concept of the
ancients as a source of wisdom. And I reveal that I am
now drawing from cultures and religions beyond
western Christianity.

The idea of the ancients I discovered in the I
Ching, and it echoed the Aboriginal concept of being in
constant contact with ancient wisdom. This is what the
elders do – stay in touch. Having said that, I think we
all have the concept of ancient wisdom somewhere
within us. It is latent in all of us. It's just a question of
how it comes out, and what cloth we choose to dress it
in, within our cultural patterns and rationales. The
scientist, the Christian and even Chicken Little, all
have their own way of admitting the ancients.

After seeing the film *Easy Rider*, I noted that for
one stream in the hippie realm, the notion of the
ancients was quite romantic. For them, there was a
literal time when life was perfect, and here they were
now, trying to get back there to that perfect time, the
Garden of Eden. Joni Mitchell even said it, in her
Woodstock song – "We've got to get ourselves back to
the garden".

Ironically, my hesitation about signing up to this
utopian vision was about tools. That group of hippie
farmers in *Easy Rider* used tools. They were hand tools
– hoes, seed spreaders, grindstones – and I guess they

would have said that the defining feature was that they didn't rely on electricity, so they didn't create the necessity for power stations and nation-wide grids of power lines. But, logical mind says: the tools still have to be made, and there is no organic, non-powered way to make steel tools. So there is a flaw in the whole bucolic vision.

And another thing: eventually you have to ask, why is it that, in the whole evolutionary development of tools across thousands of years, a certain point in time is selected as the time when everything was perfect and in balance, say, in 1600 or whenever it was that we had functional hoes and horse-drawn wagons?

I got to this slowly, I must say. When I first went bush and started a garden, I wanted to do everything by hand. This was not a bad thing, because I learned the elements, I learned the feel of soil, and because there were no machines, I learned the sound of a garden, in the morning, at midday, in late afternoon.

In many ways life was hard. We had little money, and having rejected "mainstream society", we had few ways of getting money, and it was clear that we still needed some. Even to buy hand tools you need money, and you have to drive to the shops to buy them, in a car that costs money to run, and more money to fix. This was worrying, and often gruelling and humiliating.

In these later years, it would be easy to look back and only see the hardship. But I leaf through poetry from those years and I find this, written on a scrap of paper, carefully, in black ink:

Just want you to know,
Just want you to see,
How strong it can flow:
How good it can be.

And I remember that in writing it, I wasn't addressing it to a lady, I was addressing it to the whole world. I was saying that the bliss lies in being among the things of the earth and being at peace with that.

6

Meredith and I lived in a tent for six months. It was along the top of a ridge, among forest. It took twenty minutes for the Land Rover to climb down the dirt track from there to the "main road" in the valley, and another half hour to get to town. It was fine for me – I was escaping from horror. I think Meredith was just accompanying me in my exile, and found it hard. Eventually loyalty was not enough.

It was a community. I use the term loosely. It was several hundred hectares that was owned jointly, in what was called a multiple occupancy, through a trust. There were about twenty trustees, consisting of a few families, a few couples and a few single people. But people didn't live together. We lived in our own abodes in our own nooks, spread out over the land and isolated from each other. People were looking for isolation, not communality. The talk about community was mostly just talk. We did a few things together out of necessity, like fixing the road; we all needed the road.

There was one event that served as the defining moment for Meredith and me on the multiple occupancy. We had our temporary tent erected at the bottom of a long slope, below the top of the ridge. We were getting a larger tent made. One day we had been to town, Meredith and I and our two young girls, and we came back to find an enormous log had crashed into our tent, smashing a lot of things inside and tearing one wall of the tent down. It turned out that a few of the lads had been working on splitting the log for fence posts at the top of the slope and it had got away from them.

It had rolled all the way down the slope, and as these things happen, it steered itself straight into the middle of our tent. Later, one of the lads expressed the view that they hadn't really wanted us to pitch our tent there anyway. To their credit, they had heaved the log back out of the tent, but that's kind of where the assistance ended. Meredith and I cleaned up the broken things and did the best we could to restore order. At least it was early spring and it wasn't raining. At least we hadn't been in the tent when the log rolled down.

But any hope we had had in the long-term viability of us in this "community" drained out of us that day. Hope went cold. Our new tent turned up in the next few days. That was exciting. We moved further up along the ridge, further away from everyone, and I built a wooden floor up off the ground, and we erected the new tent on top of that. It was fantastic. We had our old furniture around us, the double bed erected, the two girls across from us in their cots in the big green space that the tent created. We lived at the edge of a small pasture, a place where few people came.

It was crazy, of course. There was no water, the access was awful, and it was too far away from anyone. I had to bring water up from the valley in the Land Rover in a 44-gallon drum. On the other hand it was also exactly what I had intended to do – to get as far away as possible from the city and the feeling of revulsion it had left me with. But how would the girls meet other children? How would Meredith meet other women? How would I make a living, insofar as we were not self-sufficient? It was doomed from the start.

But I tried. I wanted this to work. And I wanted to be right here. I loved the shape of the sky here, amidst the circle

21

of trees. It was so high you could appreciate distance. You knew that a long way down, maybe an hour's worth of clambering down through the bush, you would come to a cool, clear creek, with running water, rocks, pools, shade. Water that no one had sullied or even seen.

You knew that far across the ridges there was a town, and beyond that, others. And the ocean. And far, far away, cities, all that I never wanted to have anything to do with again. I worked hard, at digging a garden, at building a shed and constructing a fence around the garden, with my poor skills and materials found at the tip, in farmers' paddocks or on the side of the road. But I took moments too, to breathe, to ponder, to appreciate the forest around me, to wonder that here I was, in the midst of it, in silence. And I wrote. During this time, only poems. No essays, no articles, no thought of publishing. I offer you samples because it is my only history of that time, and really, after so many years, it is that aspect of the time that I want to share.

This is "Song for adopted land".

Here where the clouds
tear themselves open on the trees,
or in the high distance
white ladies in gowns
hasten on secret missions,
here I'll lay out my anchor
and with love tend my acre.

When my saw bites the trunk
it spits out the smell of twenty years
and five minutes later its story
is bared in the grains,
the smooth face, the pale, perfect-formed

memory of years lush and lean –
standing again it will peer down
to soak up new life from the kitchen's corner –
and I slowly sink into the eddy
of currents that move here.

Powers on the hill:
the sun draws its own (light to light),
the water finds its level
and on the shoulders of the plants
the earth climbs into the wind

And I in the shelter of a rock for the storm-times,
run when the clouds clear
in the sheer grace of sunlight.

I'm looking back now. We didn't last long on the mountain. Six months. Meredith took the girls to visit her mother, and when I took the journey to town to ring her, she said she wouldn't come back to me unless we moved out of there, to somewhere that wasn't so remote, and in a house that had electricity. She'd found it too hard. It was a blow. My whole concept of the future was tied to that spot on the top of the mountain. I now had a thriving garden, even in the absence of a decent water supply (the weather had been kind). I had built a shed. I had scrounged a water tank from a farmer. I'd even bought a slow combustion stove, from the local timber mill owner, and transported it all the way up the mountain. I'd built a goat yard and bought a milking goat.

Meredith reasoned with me. She said all the obvious things, about the remoteness, the girls, the lack of water. And the dysfunctionality of the community. She described what I was doing as selfish.

I had to think about it. Her ultimatum brought everything unstuck. This was the end-point of my flight from the city, from mainstream culture. Here I was, at the end of a barely perceptible track along a ridge top, among a mountain range, all the way up a mountain, a long way from structures and institutions, crowds, streets and traffic, commotion and consumption. I was holding on to the dream of creating an alternative way of living, of being.

And yet the outcome was never in doubt. I had to relent. Meredith said we could find another place to do all the things I wanted to do. It didn't have to be this hard. I could have a garden, we could find a place where I could keep the goat. But she needed a house for herself and the children. I had to face it. Tom, one of the members of the community, suggested a nearby town on the other side of the range where I might find something suitable. And I did. I found a house on a farm, about fifteen miles out of the town. It was the second house on the farm, and it was right next to the first house, so it didn't feel so isolated. At the same time, it was near the end of a valley and there were no other houses within sight.

The fields were more open, although the hillsides were near and were tree-covered. The road to town was a bit rough, but it didn't require a four-wheel drive vehicle to make the trip, and it only took thirty minutes. And it had electricity. It was enough of civilisation – normal life – for Meredith to agree to come back. There was a bonus too. The owner said he could get the loan of a rotary hoe and I could have half an acre next to the house for a garden. And he kept his word, turning up with an impressive tractor-mounted rotary hoe and ploughing it all up for me, no charge. I found enough old fence posts lying around, and some old barbed wire, to fence it off and start a vegetable garden.

It was all excitement for the girls. A new house, an old couple next door who were the caretakers of the farm, and an old dairy across the road. The caretaker had a cow that he milked every morning, and I had a small yard where I kept my goat and milked her. Not that the caretaker liked the goat. He hated it. But he tolerated it. He thought we were weird – young people out here who weren't beef farmers. I had long hair and a beard, and we didn't even eat meat. But there was grudging mutual respect that grew between us, for all that.

7

And here the story could have ended. Young man gets disenchanted with city, moves to bush. After a false start, finds suitable place to settle, and settles down with wife and kids. But that's not how it went, that's never how it was likely to have gone. Why not? Well, it depends when you answer that question. In the short term, I found a job as a teacher. Okay. We looked around for a property to buy, and found a lovely place in another valley, with all the things we wanted – good water supply, decent house, electricity, close to the road, not too far from town, plenty of land and bush, sheds, even a yard for the goat. All good.

But Meredith eventually found her way to go. I think the out-of-town life was not for her. She eventually found her way back to living in a town. I hadn't wanted that. Another interesting thing about her life after our marriage was that she found religion. Not so very surprising, as she had dabbled in various options over the years, but I wonder if it was the community that attracted her. I think the disappointment in our venture in the "commune" wasn't just mine. I think she had wanted something from it too, not just on my behalf.

In the house that we had moved to, I felt very much at home. It summoned up the words of that John Denver song: "Coming home to a place he'd never seen before". I was grounded, my feet were in touch with the soil. I could breathe in. And there was the promise of a community of sorts; not a real "commune" where people lived in the same building and cooked food together, but sharing goods, helping each other and enjoying gatherings. Lots of other people our age were moving into the valley, putting up sheds to live in, planning a house and planting a garden. It seemed we had the same values and ideals. Other children were starting to arrive too. But that's me talking. I don't think Meredith saw it like that. She was gone within twelve months, taking the children with her.

That was another bright dream extinguished. Failure. I (we) had left the city with so much yearning, so much desire to find kindred spirits and build a new community, based on living in harmony with the earth. The two girls had arrived, one after the other, and that just fuelled the desire more, to find a place, to find a people, who understood what was wrong with the culture in which we had been raised, and who were attuned to nature and community. Against that vision, many of the people we encountered seemed anarchic, lazy, crazy, paranoid, indulgent, needy, greedy, selfish, hypocritical. In short, nothing like what I had envisaged, and everything I thought we were leaving behind.

Things sink in slowly, and you have to look in between the lines to see the distinctions between what people say and what they do, and then what actually happens. For there was no shortage of talk, about alternative communities, and sharing, about self-sufficiency, about an alternative economy based on bartering. About festivals, and markets. It took me a while to see that there was no single vision in all this. It was a single vision in my mind, but among the people I encountered, one person might have a focus on a particular aspect, like gardening, another person might be dedicated to alternative power sources, someone else wanted to establish an ashram, or a school. But it wasn't just this, it was the fact that people were driven by different and often opposing ideas, and everyone carried so much from the culture we had supposedly rejected.

"We had brought it all with us." That's the thought that dropped into my mind sometime after arriving in the valley. The next thought was a bit more difficult to allow: "So had I". If I was looking at this band of new settlers and thinking, "I don't like what I see, in terms of the likelihood that we will build a viable, positive alternative to the mainstream culture", then some other new settlers were probably looking at me thinking the same thing. That was much harder. It opened up two sets of questions for me. One set of questions was, "How do I get a clearer picture of myself? What mental models are there that will help me to get a better understanding of myself? How do I become a better, wiser person?"

The second set of questions I was faced with was, "How do I judge other people? Do I make judgements at all? How can I live among people when I have feelings of disgust, anger, et cetera, or delight and respect, about what they do?" This realisation of the deep questions I had no answers for challenged me. The dream of being part of building an alternative community was crumbling. It pained me and distressed me. I thought for a while that the answer was to be more discerning. It was just that I hadn't found the right people yet. I had to get better at weighing up "where people were coming from".

But it didn't seem to work out that way. No great visionaries appeared, no leaders. And here was a big, new factor: I was no longer geographically mobile. I had found my home, and whatever was going to happen, it had to be with that fact in mind: it had to happen from here. And I did find people around the valley and around the district that I had things in common with. I learned that I didn't have to accept everyone, I could choose not to associate with some people. From the present time, this sounds as if I had been dreadfully naïve. I want to stop and go back and express it differently. But I'll leave it. If I want to look into this experience and see what sense I make of it now, I have to look at it raw.

Still there was that yearning to bring everyone in, to make everyone part of the new world. The new community was the seed of a new way, to stand against the ugliness, greed and corruption of the mainstream society. One day, when I was living on the mountain, I was walking, naked in the sun and the fresh air of a spring morning, along the top of the ridge, looking far down into the valley with its distant paddocks and fences, trees and cows, the creek threading its way through the middle, when an F111 fighter plane flew past me, close, at high speed. In fact, it was below me, wrapping its way along the contours of the hills. It was close enough that I could have seen the pilot if I'd had time. It was past me before I heard anything at all, then there was the deafening boom of the sound barrier breaking. I stood in contrast, grateful to be powerless, not wanting to win such a contest.

Another time on the mountain, a group of us had been right down into the second valley for a gathering. Afternoon swims in a shady pool, food, meeting new arrivals and people who lived even further out than we

28

did. Afterwards, walking the long walk back up the hill, and looking across the other side of the gully, into bushes and forest that had never been logged. The general truth was that everywhere had been logged at least once since white men had arrived in this area about one hundred years ago.

But there were pockets of untouched bush, and I looked straight into the heart of this particular pocket. I saw its ancient self, fecund, endlessly reaching up and exuding radiance. I saw in its deep green a writhing heart that was always materialising, always exuberant, tireless, joyful. It was a gift moment, a revealed secret. Who are we to presume on this planet?

I wrote this poem while I was on the mountain: "Gifts of Dawn":

Awaken to the day;
night, the healing dark,
has chewed to soft juice
the stalks and weeds
of fears and untasted hopes.

Yesterday would,
in the grey approaching dawn,
be only a thief.

But the bird who is
a door chime to the day,
the clouds that remark
the delicate transition of light,
and the crown down
the earth-wide hallway,
His Majesty the Sun:
all these are givers
and the golden flower that bursts
on the thick-scented horizon
to grace the night's gift of dew
says to start here –

already bright and clear,
surrounded by unstinting lovers –
and head for the zenith.

It probably strives too much for metaphors, but what I see in it now is the central idea that all our striving, as humans, each one and all together, is embraced by the arms of the earth, it is located in the cradle of nature. We come from earth and we return to it, and our communities will not prosper if they reject this truth. Perhaps this is the one necessary thing that the hippie search for a new way of living offered to the world.

8

That is me thinking now. Back then, I just knew that the dream was breaking up before it had come to anything viable. I never took that to be a political or general fact; it was simply what was happening with me. I hadn't been able to find, or create, any congenial kind of community. I was having to go back and reconceive what it was I was looking for.

Meredith and I had only been in the valley for a few months when she became pregnant again. It seemed fitting: a new child to fill out our family in our new home. Her pregnancy went well, and her belly grew larger than before. Both the girls had been small at birth, so this was a fine thing. And then it happened, that at birth it turned out there were two babies. Twins. Two boys. A monumental surprise.

Nowadays people find this hard to believe. How could you not know? Couldn't the doctor tell? Didn't she have a scan done? No; scans were an unusual thing then. But I don't have to explain. I don't have to tell the doctor's story, or Meredith's story or anyone else's. I am just telling the story of how it was, how it happened. Two babies were born. So we had four children, not three.

I can tell you the words that were said. When Meredith had delivered the first baby, the doctor said, "I think there's another one there." That's what was said. And I can remember the breath that I took and what I said in reply, "Well, I suppose it had better come out then." With a wry smile. Four is more than three, but it wasn't as if we weren't already a family.

My eldest daughter can remember when I told her and her sister that two babies had been born. She remembers what a staggering idea that was to her as a three-year-old. She didn't quite understand what it meant. It certainly meant a sudden upgrade in goods – the brooding awareness that the fridge was in its last days, and also the car, became urgencies, and we bought a bigger fridge, and a bigger car that promised to be reliable. The nursery had to accommodate two bassinets instead of one; we needed more nappies, more baby clothes.

The girls took to it. Two girls and two baby brothers. Neighbours came to help, with washing, cooking, care. But Meredith was deflated, tired. No matter how much I tried, we tried, everyone tried, she was not happy. I said, "This may be a hard time, but it will get easier". And in truth, I thought we had come apart too. Months before the boys were born, I wrote this poem about our differences.

The winding way

No, you were never one for listening,
and I was never one for talking.
I think you have your ideas about love,

31

but I grew in a different way...
I have loved you through mists and confusion,
reeled through starless nights
scratching fuel from anywhere handy
to keep going.
There I learned the pathways of darkness:
do I trip on your bright dreams?
(And I know it would help
if we understood,
but there is that need again.)
I watch you plunge, and plunge,
I hold out against the ideas
and do no good.
You fade into mists again,
you give me opinions,
want words,
when all I ever said was
"Come along"
and excused the emptiness
because it never is...
happy that way,
love you.

And you could ask yourself, was I saying that I
was actually happy with the unhappiness, or was I
simply resigning myself to it? There is another phrase
that has appeared in my work more than once: "Each
our own way we must go to the desert, where the
angels will minister to us". There is something of that
thought in here. It is not a neat answer, and not
altogether clear what it might mean. But sometimes
that it how it is to our consciousness, and we must
accept all of the facets, the ambiguity.

In Robert Heinlein's *Stranger in a Strange Land*,
he invented the word "grokking", which expresses the
"gestalt" concept as a verb: we experience
transformation when we embrace everything we are in

the midst of – we "get it". But mostly we don't want to "grok" it all; we want instant solutions, and generally it turns out that they only ever address part of the problem. I know there is an accepted wisdom nowadays that the main problem with man-woman relationships is that men are unable to express their feelings, and women want to express their feelings.

I simply suggest that this is a very circumscribed truth. It is neither universally true of men nor of women, and as the "solution" for relationship problems it is often not desirable or helpful. Not everything needs to be said, and indeed, some things are killed off in being put into words. We seem to have forgotten this. Sometimes people talk in order to camouflage something, or to distract you from it, not to reveal it or be honest about it. And sometimes people talk without having any consciousness of what the problem is. All of this.

In retrospect, I would say, Meredith and I had run our course with each other. I would have preferred to continue; I had a strong commitment to the family, and to being a father to my children. But Meredith would have had another view about that, about what her commitment was, and what mine was. In looking at the past, there are some things it is useful to explore and "get to the bottom of", and it is just as true that there are some things that are best left in peace, in all their ambiguity.

What I do have in my poems are some indications about myself around that time. There was the personal and there was the political/social. I think the problem I had, and which was shared by many of the new settlers – the visionaries, I mean, not the escapees – was that I thought I could find or create a social/economic solution to the problems of society while assuming that the personal/family life would proceed unproblematically. Well, not entirely. I just have to write this and refine it as I go.

Yes, "we" wanted to reshape life completely – schools and food and gardens and living with nature, and go back to a more tribal existence where seasonal festivals meant something. And of course this meant reshaping family life, for the majority of us who weren't living in a "real" commune. So I think what we underestimated is how deeply this would require us to go in personal exploration, and how much it would challenge our conceptions of ourselves, and how confronting this would be. Oh yes, we could all *say* that it would be confronting, and that we were ready for it, but knowing what this meant in practice was something else.

In practice it meant encountering fear, rage, anger, depression and abandonment in ourselves. Unpredictably, because although there was a loose common ideal on the horizon, where we were coming from was quite different for each of us, and I think that few of us understood this, or the depth of it. So in families, we just thought we would carry on smoothly.

In short, Meredith left. The twins were just ten months old. She left a note: "I am going. I have the children." I had not been ready for this.

I found this poem. The date on it is just two weeks before our first child was born.

Bustling

I am a rose bush,
all tangle and thorns.
A long way down it is
to any solid wood.
The silent, pure heart
has to wait out storms,
bustling in the wind,
as if life were there,

as if the lost could give directions
    and not rat mazes,
as if the desert could yield
water instead of dust,
as if thorns could bring
    delight to eye and touch.
Not here the power
or the succour:
come inside and rest,
let the waves roll to
listless, lapping foam,
thorns shrivel and die.
Let go the little buffets of anger,
and move from the stillness only.

What would you say? I was a person who experienced anger and frustration? I was looking for direction and not finding it? How much of this anger was social/political and how much personal? There are such arguments between these two camps. "They're different things." "No they're not; one is a reflection of the other." "We have to change the system. The personal is the political." We've had it all.

But it's one thing to get the theory right; it's quite another to know what it means in practice, in your own life. It is difficult to accept the complicated ways in which the personal and the political interconnect. Some of those threads are direct, but some of them go way back into the life of cultures and societies, into Jung's collective unconscious.

One of my greatest lessons in those connections was when I was writing *The Ten Thousand Things*, and throwing the I Ching while I was writing. There were two streams of the story, one personal and one grounded in an organisation. I was alternating the chapters, thinking that one was counterpoint and respite from the other. And then, as the two streams developed, separately, I threw exactly the same coins twice – once when I was writing about the organisation, and a second time when I was writing about the personal relationship. That's three coins thrown six times in each case. The odds are thousands to one against that happening.

The same streams are working underground. I couldn't have had a more emphatic lesson than in that throw of the coins. But I had taken the family as my refuge. I had wanted it as the bulwark against the ugliness of the world, as many people do. But perhaps it was that this attitude just became an unfair burden on the family (and Meredith). This poem dates from a few months before the twins were born.

Such distances

Out on the road
the cars are forever passing –
roadblocks, strikes and higher prices

When we take our weekly trip into town
we make it a smooth ride for the children
and when the papers
turn to violence or to sex
we no longer blaze
with pressure-group zeal

Our daughter is two:
she stares straight into your eyes
until you see the point
where it's okay

But they say a missile
can be commissioned to targets
from farther than the magis' months of travel,
travel which to young daughters
is a ride on daddy's shoulders,

36

a sleep in the car,
or dreams at night

They say from closets of concrete,
terror taunts such distances.
Here we have an entirely new
and serious situation –
battle without the whites of eyes
and without interludes

Our daughter's eyes are blue
(I wonder if you have ever seen such blue)
they are clearer and quite bolder
than they should be
for the little time that they have spent
and the horrors that may already have been sent.
Then, we shall see...

But suddenly there was no family. I would walk around
the house, looking into the empty rooms.

9

It took some time for this event to work its way through
my being. I went to work (I was teaching at a school now), I
looked after my garden, I painted the kitchen. I read the I
Ching, and befriended King Wen through Richard Wilhelm's
translation – from Chinese into German, and then Cary
Baynes did the translation into English, and it was first
published in English, fittingly, I thought, in the year of
my birth. I was learning the thoughts of the ancients,
and even what King Wen had to say about the ancients.

The dream of the new way receded for a time. I
had hurt to mend. I wrote this poem for a friend whose
love affair had ended a year or two before Meredith left

me. But I read it now and I think it serves well to describe my own subsequent experience.

The after days

A plane will streak across the laden sky,
I will hear the car halt outside
and the doorbell ring:
She will be there.

The birds start another day,
singing always only clear joy;
sun streams suddenly
at another awakening.

Inside I am as dry as drought,
hopes a brief dewy layer over wiltedness;
day rises like wind –
I torn as birds' nests undefended.

The shadows of other days spread
and search me out like
cold fingers, or fishermen's nets –
remembering the full sun,
first-time feelings,
warmth and boldness of love.

Then
the distance she drew
to her untidy good-bye,
the roar of pain

Eyes   see   room
chair   table   cup
sit
fill time with
fragments of living
begin to wash clothes

begin to sweep
pour cold coffee down sink
tidy

If I ever see her,
by chance in a house of friends
or on a street,
it will cause no hurt,
for she will be someone else
and I....

There are phrases I remember from my poems. They come back to me in the present. "Move from the stillness only" is a deep lesson that I am still learning. "For she will be someone else, and I..." also comes back to me occasionally. I find great promise in it, and the forgiveness of time. I don't mean her forgiving me, or my forgiving her, I mean the universe forgiving all of us and giving us new days, to start again and be good creators.

King Wen says, when the traveller has no place to shelter, proceed humbly. Follow the wind. Then regret vanishes. Look for what is proper between Heaven and Earth. The Irish writer, John O'Donohue, also recognises the traveller in us: "The person is always a nomad, journeying from threshold to threshold, into ever different experiences. In each new experience, another dimension of the soul unfolds" (from his lovely book, *Anam Cara*).

For a time, I read very few books other than some novels and the I Ching. I discovered Tom Robbins and his joyous, wicked quirkiness, in *Even Cowgirls Get the Blues*. I was full of, that is, finished with, books and thinking. I'd had enough, I had to be doing things with my hands. And now I think, from this vantage point, after the failure of the alternative lifestyle to prove achievable at a level that has made any discernible difference to mainstream society, even if this is so, there were things of value. Even, simply, that men and women did significant things with their hands, generally without any prior knowledge or experience.

I had been hopeless with saws and hammers growing up. I was an intellectual, with my head in books. And I think that was true for most of "us" new settlers. But I learned to plan and build sheds, to split logs and build fences (straight and taut), to create a garden and produce magnificent vegetables. I wonder how many of the general populace, city-bound, know the joys and frustrations, the exigencies, of making something in the natural world, tuning into materials and other forms of life, working with them, taming them and being tamed by them.

Learning the one great truth we all learned, without exception: that every major project is going to take four times as long as you first think it will. And the second great truth: that once you've started, you have to keep going until it is finished, and keep one eye on the weather. It was in the doing of such things that I slowly changed. I expressed the endeavour this way.

Small deaths

What is right for you
is all that will do,
no books, or rules, or knowledge
will stand where you must,
in the spotlight of trust,
working calmly and strong in your image.

No precedents ease,
no approvals appease
the self that lies waiting to grow;
with illusions it strives,
midst confusion survives,

unsuspected, it haunts 'til you know.

But when you stand centre-stage,
you read clear as a gauge,
and move with a freedom that's power;
small rewards that you cherished
will soon have all perished
in the struggle and glory of the hour.

What's right for you
is all that will do,
not 'til then are you any man's brother.
Find the self that is lost,
turn away from the cost –
your true life has small deaths for its mother.

To myself, I saw it as having to give up. Having to give up on dreams. Of the hope of community, of the security of family. Perhaps that was what was wrong with me, I thought – the hanging onto dreams. One must live without any dreams. Give them all up – the ideals of family, communes and communities, alternative economics. Not to give up on the practice, but to give up the dreams. The dreams were just expectations that burdened our experience unrealistically.

Now it seems melodramatic, to be excused, perhaps, by my sense of shock and disappointment at the various setbacks and turns of event. But I had time to think. And I think Meredith resented that. I think she saw herself as having to take on the whole burden, with the children, and I was the one that got lucky. But I thought that that thought was a hole anyone could disappear into. I hadn't made the choice, I had been the recipient of it. Now I would live my new life as best I could. Bereft but still able.

As King Wen said, "Dealing with a difficult situation, attitude is important". There are many situations. Mountain means "keeping still". Sitting in stillness is nourishing to the spirit. So I dug my garden, mulched it and kept out the weeds. Radish grew, and silver beet, tomatoes, corn, beetroot, lettuce, cucumbers, beans zucchinis. Most of it I gave away, and for a time the health food store in town would take baskets of vegetables from me.

I was now sitting between camps. I wasn't a hippie because I lived in a house that had electricity. I had a job, or numerous jobs in succession, each of which changed my relationship to the local mainstream community, but all of which made me part of it, even the role of coordinating the adult education program for the district. I was melding two cultures, in a modest way. Woodwork and computer skills on one side, massage and stained glass on the other. But which side was which? It became so it was hard to tell, which was the whole point. "Straight" people joined the alternative courses, and new settlers participated in the "normal" courses.

Always I wanted something that seemed to be just out of reach. There is a recent song where the lady sings, wryly, "I think I was made for longing". I understood what the lady meant. Sometimes, it seemed, all I had was that sense of longing. I wrote more poems to assuage the longing.

Reminder

Reminder –
to press hard,
to squeeze the last drop of truth
from truth's orange.
And people most of all,
and most of all one's self
can lose the tightness, the majesty

of being one and high.
Straighten, then
(reminder) –
this is always the moment that is required,
when we seize steps
to lay hold of our destiny.
Fear the mind-killer
must yield to freedom;
the crack is in the wall,
the promise of light
races to the corner of our weakness,
to tease us to brightness.
Gone be the grey light,
disband the sadly amusing
spectacle of our poor lives.
Now let the angels watch us,
heart and mind and soul,
stream home to the goal.

And out of all that tortuousness I remember "heart and mind and soul – stream home to the goal". But while that was the urge, in reality, I was but at the beginning of another transit, a long journey in this place. Indeed I was at the beginning of a different story. I became conscious of living in a valley, and what it might mean. It is only recently that I discovered John O'Donohue (of *Anam Cara*); he has something to say about living in a valley: "To live in a valley is to enjoy a private sky. All around, life is framed by the horizon. The horizon shelters life, yet constantly calls the eye to new frontiers and possibilities."

Yes, I can attest to what he says. I have been in places that are crossroads, or saddles between two valleys, and the energy is different. It is dissipated, transient, both furtive and brash. When you entered the valley where I lived you came in as if through a doorway. There was a point where the cliffs came in close, so once you kept going, you were inside, and everyone who lived there was with you, even if you seldom saw them. Whatever they were, they were your brethren. In trouble you were their neighbour, and they yours. It was quite clear.

Given that I had the most established house of all the new settlers, a house with floors and walls and a rain-proof (more or less) roof, and electricity and running water (courtesy of the ever-flowing spring and the rainwater tanks, and the previous farmer's one hundred metres of piping), I was often the refuge in flood times. People slept in my lounge room, or they came after the storms to get their clothes washed in my washing machine and dry out. And I had a telephone, another luxury, so people came to make phone calls.

What is important to remember after all this time? Sitting on the verandah, hearing the creek murmur and bubble just twenty metres away, maybe five or six of us. Grass steaming in that bright sun that appears after a flood, the kettle boiling on my slow combustion stove for tea. Languid, precious time. Respecting that desire we each had, in some way, to make something good of our lives. We had all come from places in the city, both physically and figuratively. We had all been disappointed, or found it much harder than we had naively expected. We had all come from traumas and rebellion, and now we had to make something, we had to put rebellion aside.

10

I had time, on my own, to let writing happen, not just poems. I started to write stories. I had tried when I was younger, but they were so stilted that I gave them up. I was still reticent, but I wrote and wrote, and sometimes felt that

I got the stance right. It's that saying of Archimedes: give me the right place to stand, and my lever will lift the world (yes, I know, not quite right; my version of the moment). I had never wanted to be one of those savage writers who prey upon reality, who use it just as fodder. There are many stories I won't tell because it would be taking too many liberties with other people's lives.

So I looked for ways to tell stories that drew from my experience without dishonouring people. I made names for characters that suggested worlds that might speak to our hearts, that might connect with strangers across space and time. I was not expecting readers to map entire worlds, as Tolkein and Ursula Le Guin and Frank Herbert have done. I just wanted to disorient people enough to enable them to look at my characters and their happenings with fresh eyes.

"Prevailing myths" was one of my efforts. "Krauwing stood on the edge of the world. All he could see was a multitude of places where he could fall. He waited for the fall, which didn't come." That's how it starts. So I'm thinking, I will do this: I will put some stories at the end of this book. It will take some doing. Many of them were written before personal computers were invented. Imagine that! I had a manual typewriter during my first few years in the valley, and I typed my stories, page by page, with "white-out" to correct my (many) mistakes. When I wanted copies, I photocopied them on a photocopier in town.

So I may need to retype them. And yes, I have thought about scanning them into the computer, but the type is so light and fuzzy that the scanner won't recognise the words. So it goes.

Krauwing is where the crack in the wall comes from. Or perhaps the poem above came first. I don't remember. Krauwing lives with a jaded realism: when you see a crack in a wall, make sure someone else sees it too before you mention it. Then they will like you.

Don't even mention it then. Let them say, "Hey, did you see this crack in the wall?" and be pleased about it. But Krauwing encounters a lady, and she whispers in his ear, "One doesn't always just look through gaps in the wall." So he learns lessons that are more life-enhancing. The prevailing myths change.

King Wen says the situation I am thinking about is one caused by predecessors. It is the evil done by parents that is manifested in their children. It is ruined, decayed. And to take on this situation is to inherit the duty of caring for the people. My eyes open wide again. Why? I think of the hippie commune in *Easy Rider*, and the simple-minded veneration in which they hold the ancestors. But wait. Aren't the ancestors also the source of the delusions and corruption? So which ancestors are which?

I come in and out of this symbolic world, at times bewildered, at times pierced by its seeming accuracy, even when the imagery seems obscure. The seemingness is resonant, it echoes with moments. The traditional image of corruption is a vase containing the five poisonous creatures: snake, scorpion, centipede, gecko and toad. They were put into a jar together until one had killed and eaten all the others. The venom which ensued could craze and kill a victim and secure his goods for the perpetrator of the magic. And magic is such a temptation in our age – the magic of technological power.

And what does King Wen offer in the face of the spell? To see the connection between personal disorders and cultural change. To reconnect with the primal powers. To confront the problems of individual identity, sexuality and personal identity or mission. Which is to say, in some sense, you already know what is needed. Not as a grand plan, no, but situation by situation, moment by moment if necessary.

The revolution had failed. It did not transpire. But there was a reason. The path is different. It is much longer, but it leads all the way to the source. The earth was not ready. Everyone needs to be there. You need to live your story, your own story, in all its seeming insignificance. It will take bliss, and pain, and cups of tea on the verandah.

11

I have built a memorial tablet to the ancestors;
In fact I have built rather a lot.

And my children came back. After weeks during which I heard nothing, and I contemplated that I might never see them again, Meredith's car came up the drive. I was in the yard, putting clothes on the line in the sunshine. The car pulled up, and a door opened, and my two girls ran across to me, as fast as their little legs could carry them. They hugged me around the legs, hard. It was a moment in which the world stopped, and turned about. It was a moment of deep knowing. I knew that I was their father, forever, as I always had been. How foolish I had been to doubt that.

It did not matter about time or distance, and clearly, there was no doubt in their minds. In that moment I decided that it did not matter what would happen at a practical level in the subsequent years, I would consciously and constantly be their father, and the father of the twins. And when they were grown they would know that this had been so. This was my decision. Whatever else has changed in my life, it has shaped itself around this core.

King Wen would have called it fixing the omens. It made everything else easier, to know myself as father, as an incontrovertible fact. Perhaps I was not much present in their lives, and in that way I was ineffectual, but I don't doubt the importance of my decision, for them as much as for myself. It allowed me to invest myself in the life I was being given, rather than being disconsolate or grudging. It meant that I could adventure, lightly. Whatever there was to learn and to understand, it was better done with joy than sorrow.

Over the water

Over the water,
the wind has arisen;
bleak nights and good days rustle together.
I understand day by day,
and do you go away?

The light grows / things continue to happen
The tide flows / we stand still
The wind bends us together
We touch on what is good
before retreating.

Over the water
the wind is singing,
I listen to its rise and fall,
rise and fall.
I watch,
and the movement is in the light.
Satisfied again
day by day.

"Rambril first met Shar in the garden." So began another story ("Rambril's story"), which I am going to put at the end of the book. I know this is okay, because Herman Hesse did it at the end of *The Glass Bead Game*.

I have to trust my stories to supply me with facts, for Shar became important for a time. Was it in her garden that we first met? There is no reason to trust my stories; I just made them up. Yes, they contained salient facts, but the formulation might be in the service of convenience or art. The focus was the story.

Shar was precious and yet carried a suggestion of danger. In those days, my measure was how people located themselves against the ideal of the alternative, personally, spiritually, socially, economically. Her stance was very particular, and offered without apology. She was a midwife. She delivered babies in remote homes in the hills. She dealt with life and death, and she knew it. She had her devotees and her assailants.

She was no saint who lived above emotions. In anger she smashed a window and cut herself. (Strangely, Meredith had done the same thing, I learned from my children.) I don't pretend to have fathomed this episode, about which I knew little. I knew from what she said that she was conscious of the power of her anger.

Shar arrived in the valley in the company of two men. It was remarked upon. People had questions, and theories. There was a son, but whose son? They lived in a tent down by the creek, until they moved into an old house, one that had seemed abandoned, but someone had bought it recently. Then they moved up onto a ridge, and configurations reconfigured. One man left, the other built her a house. She lived there by herself, just with the children. Yes, there were three children now. Mystery and good works were her core qualities.

Our paths intersected in the wake of Meredith's departure. Drinking tea on her verandah in the afternoon, massaging her after an all-night delivery of a baby, her bringing her kids to my place when my kids were visiting, when my sister was visiting from England. Drinking port at her house late at night, kids asleep. Hearing the unearthly scream of koalas fighting

49

in the clear night of a full moon. There were fires. She had a magnificent stone fireplace for winter. And then there was Damien, the potter, who had a wood-fired kiln that required an all-night party to fire a batch of pots.

That was a good fire. The wood was gathered for weeks. Everyone knew there would be a firing at full moon. The kiln had to get to a certain temperature, and Damien would be frantic, watching the thermometer, and coaxing the men to keep feeding the fire, to get that temperature up. Amid wine, and cannabis, and bountiful food, all flowing. Laughter, the moon in the sky, and Damien in his element, frantic but focused, thinking of his pots. A long way from the jungles of Vietnam, and the helicopters flying over bringing death to those beneath.

I sink and sink and sink, into the texture of the valley and all it brings me. Not trying to press it into the shape of a revolution or an ideal. You just have to be where you are. I don't say I ever did this with complete integrity or mastery, but I renewed my faith each day. I wonder if Damien "made it", as they say. He was distressed. In summer time the helicopters would fly over, low, looking for cannabis crops. It was a sport the police engaged in annually. What fun it was, to get together a team and raid the encampments in the hills, and triumphantly seize a crop and drag the ill-dressed hippies into the courts.

What I know is that every time there was the sound of a helicopter, Damien would go berserk and run away into the hills and hide. For hours. He would come cowering back to Linda after sundown, sweating and still afraid. What happened to him in Vietnam? I imagined him hunkered down underneath some bushes, a long way up in the hills, shivering. It was madness. I imagined Linda and the

50

children, shaken and worried. Would he come back? Would they go out and find him dead or mad somewhere tomorrow?

They left the valley. One time, I was going to Sydney, down to see my kids, and they said I should stop and see them. It was a tiny house, so tiny, perched right on the edge of the highway, a fast stretch where the semi-trailers roared past at top speed all night. Unnerving. They shook the whole house. Linda was doing her best, yet again, to make a home of it with the children, and Damien was still crazy, manic. At least there was music. There was that bond. Perhaps it was Crosby, Stills, Nash and Young. We held onto it. It was a place where we could make contact and he could be free, at least for a time, from the demons.

I know nothing more about Damien. When Rambril met Shar, she was with Damien and Linda. In the story, he is wounded but tenacious.

12

Shar. A story that need not be told, yet there is truth there that still holds resonance. There is music that engenders a rhythm and that is enough, it flows. There are words that might give the gist of it, of when we were in the swing of things happening, swinging sometimes over a pit, momentarily soaring high, hearing a refrain and feeling changes of mood. I come to acquiesce and move along the path, inevitably, inexorably. There was a spell, there was a high place, and we moved selflessly.

I wrote a poem about a calf. I was driving home and it was in a paddock, standing alone with its head against a post, just standing there with its head pressed against the post. It was poignant.

The calf had its head
against the fence post.
Not moving at all.
How long would it stand there?
For hours maybe.
Just like that.
But the spells of fence posts,
being time-born,
are time-worn:
tomorrow there will be a calf
who knows about
the spells of fence posts
and how to break them.

Shar and I spent time together. I'm not sure what it meant for her. Perhaps it was an exploration of someone different, to experience my particular qualities. Perhaps it was the thinking and the writing that I did. Perhaps this was not usual in her experience. But she always held her reserve, and did not lead me to expect. Yet we stood tall with each other. I painted a room in her house. I dedicated an entire room to the colour yellow. Perhaps no one would do that now. She mended clothes for me. Perhaps that would not happen today either. If so, then there was something interesting about us, and about that particular time.

She sat and read by the fire while I did careful brush strokes, hour upon hour. We didn't talk. Well, perhaps we did, but it is the silence I remember. In the afternoon, a friend of hers came to visit. Not an ordinary visit, but a crisis. A lady, a mother and three children, she confused and hurt, angry with a crazy and violent man. The children playing with Shar's two children, trying to be unaffected.

The tale is told, and there are tears, and fear – "I am trapped". Shar has no answers, only to hold her for a while, to give her the strength to get up again. To make tea for the adults, and to be practical about meals for the children. To make sure the fire is lit and there is warmth to share. The mother will get her space where she can think, and recover.

And I say to the shattered lady things like this: if there is to be peace there must be strength in the heart. Love is born in fire but the mind must be there to tame it. Passion can consume us and destroy what it touches. Our love must be mindful, steady, like the glow of the fire before which Shar reads her book in the morning when she is tired.

The only mischief the light plays is when you take your eyes off it, and then it is like the leprechaun which may perchance disappear. But kept in your sight it will show you its magic. And then you may begin again. Did I say any of this? I do not know. But all those thoughts formed in that space, amid the sadness and desperation.

Night. The children are all sleeping, in various beds. Shar has seen the day woven back into sleep and is free herself to be tired. She sits again by the fire-glow and holds her spirit steady. At a certain point I withdraw and return home, to sit by my own fire.

A disturbing thought: that it has been assumed today that Shar and I are both elders. I had always assumed that someone else would be an elder, or that there was some public process by which you came to be an elder, so that it was clear to you and everyone that this was what was happening. And, by implication, that there were publicly agreed standards by which one could know that one was becoming an elder, and what you had to do to develop your skills and standing.

All I had done was to be a seeker and adhere to the concept of ancient and continuous wisdom. I thought I had been invisible. Suddenly I felt someone was listening to me, and it would make a difference what kind of things I said. I'm not sure I was ready to take on that responsibility, even though it would be flattering to be thought wise. I think that Shar felt this too, but I think, more consciously than I, and I think it came with the territory for one who served as a midwife, who communed with the gods of life and death.

King Wen, in talking about "sojourning at the borders", talks about a zone of radical transformation, when the bright omens that guide our lives become flying words that carry them across the threshold of life and death. He says, "You must deal with Power and your responsibilities to the human community". I did not know how to respond appropriately, but what I didn't realise was that perhaps I had anyway.

What else do I remember of myself and Shar? One night, when we went from her massage class to a meeting about a constitution for a new Steiner school, I prepared potato and leek soup in a thermos. We stopped at a lookout and the full moon was rising. I poured soup into two bowls and brought out spoons and black pepper. The whole district lay below us in soft light, silent. This was enough, in our warm bellies.

Nothing else was this simple.

13

That vase with the poisonous things. King Wen's image. I wasn't done with it. He said it was about the ancestors. But I (we) wasn't just a victim, I was a product of my past. I was troubled by this image and what it meant. I read more. He said, allow what is rotting to rot away, and go back to the source. Arouse a new sense of our common needs. Work at this. It is pleasing to the spirits.

I rise early. I sit on the back step and pull on my boots. I walk down to the bridge. I do not stop, but I hear the water, bearing new secrets after the night, secrets she bears openly but in code. I keep walking, walking to the constant sound of the water. I listen; there are other moments here, moments that are yet unblessed. I rise to the occasion: I bless those moments, all moments.

Back on the step I take off wet boots, and go in to make tea. I take it out onto the verandah, because the whole world is present there. The magpie comes, cheeky, looking for breakfast. I am ready with scraps of bread. The sun shines now, as loud as a Pentecost choir. It might as well be the first time. I sit quietly while bliss explodes around me, laughter and laughter. I am not using up stores of bliss, I am adding to them.

I look through the doorways of sheds and shelters up and down the valley and beyond, hearing voices. There are battles waging, no solutions. I think: belligerent people fight. Sullen people sulk. There are always excuses to be made. On the other side of the glass, excuses are reasons. And the glass feels hard. King Wen says only that with sincerity the mind penetrates the meaning of things.

14

Into this setting, and these particular moments and people, things came to rest. The counter culture had dissolved into the moods and decisions of ordinary people, the alternative society had all but evaporated. The grand dreams were over and the small days had come. It was time to remember the starting point, and I found it back in the days before I had come to the valley. I had been in hospital after a motor bike accident, for months, immobilised and with time to think.

Lying in bed, I had written "Heaven".

"Heaven must be here someplace."
He said it, tramping along,
going down to the creek
near the old stone hut,
frost in the air
and the city a long way behind.

He said it, having time
to listen to the water bubbling,
time enough to have a plan
splash around in his head while the sun dried him.

"Heaven must be here someplace."
He wasn't even close,
was close only to the man
who was taking so long to die,
was thinking only of that painful passage
into dumbness. He said it,
somehow, in spite of being numbed,
his voice thin but hard,
in the face of all
the unfulfilled plans, the tumbling fall
from a dumb man's limp hands.
Said it: his voice coming
from far off, but lingering:

"Heaven must be here someplace."
He sat, thinking,
happiness is always in the past –
we recognise it afterwards.
And then we start again,
extract a promise from some girl
who happened to look our way twice,
and so we live,

56

rising and remembering,
false hopes and keepsakes.

"Heaven must be here someplace."
He said it, persistent.
Turn another stone, kiss the earth,
turn your face to the sun,
be as one, make
your second birth.
Eternally now, ecstatically, heaven.
Heaven, here, someplace.

It was still true, and remarkable to me that I had been so faithful to that vision in some respects, and remarkable also what I had forgotten. We had come, all of us in our own way, to build new lives. Over time, I noticed that people did this in two fundamentally different ways. Some people built their shelters and homes with salvage, and others built it up entirely new, and as much as possible out of the earth itself. It seemed to me that here were two opposite responses to the given culture.

One approach was to go back to the earth, literally, and build a house out of mud or rocks or felled timber. One of my neighbours spent about two years just gathering stones from around the valley, before he started building at all. Another neighbour felled the timber for his house off his own land, and had it transported to the local mill, where it was sawn into beams and transported back to him for his building. Then there were the two neighbours who built a mud-brick house. This involved making bricks, one by one, out of the earth on their property, thousands of bricks, day upon day, and then laying them, one on top of the other, until the house was built.

When you make your own house, and you build it out of your own raw, natural materials, you have made a powerful thing, that puts a packaged, commoditised culture in a lesser place, and at a distance. You have made your own space, and you own it in a way that no one else can know. People from the mainstream might question why one would spend all this time building their own house when they could have a job and pay someone else to do the building, and it would be so much easier, because the builders would know what they were doing at the outset.

But I understood the desire. Even though I already had a house, I did build a separate structure, a big room with a half-mezzanine floor, looking down on the space below. I rationalised it as a bedroom for the children when they visited, but it was more about having the satisfaction of building something from scratch. And the timber came from trees that I had felled on my land.

The other way of building was also intriguing to me. It was as if you were looking for the parts of the old culture that had been overlooked, and you were bringing them back to life. You were recognising value that other people couldn't see, or sometimes they could see but didn't know how to continue with. The slow combustion stove I bought when we lived on the mountain was an example. The mill owner I bought it from was pleased that I wanted it. You'd think a mill owner, of all people, would want to keep a wood-fired stove, but the wife wanted modern appliances. She figured she'd earned it after being his wife all this time. He wasn't keen about the switch; he was nostalgic. I imagine he remembered when he first installed it.

There was also an ethic attached to salvaging. It was a commitment to making use of what was already around, instead of producing more new stuff. It was a principled and heartfelt response to a wasteful culture. And to do this in clever ways, to take a piece of rubbish and see an innovative use for it, that was also a motivator. The new culture, as Roszak had observed, was at its heart playful and joyous. It aimed to amuse as well as feed, clothe and shelter people.

So there was good work happening in the valley. But the real work, in which I was still a poor student, was inner work. My work was to remember that I had to start with heaven, not hope that it would arrive when the building was finished or some other goal had been achieved. "Heaven must be here someplace" was meant to be a droll comment. It was meant to evoke an image like that of a swaggie mooching about in his swag looking for his pouch of tobacco. It had to be there somewhere. And of course, it ends up being right in front of him.

15

Going further back to see how I would go ahead, I found this poem too, from my city days.

Children

Children, we had our day,
we danced and had time to be wise.
And there are still
songs to be sung,
but the prophets
have all bought themselves
houses in the country, while we,
reeling from their ruthless logic,
are in search
of the lyricism of an older beauty,
woven of answers this time.

When I lived in the city, there were plenty of critics who could tell us all what was wrong, but they didn't seem to stay around to offer any answers. But I am being glib now, and talking old talk. I think differently now. First, I brought doubt to the idea of the "answer" – the one right thing to do. Then I thought in terms of "an answer" because perhaps there were many. And then I moved to focusing on the process of answering – that was the thing, the process was itself the answer, as long as you were unwinding the problem and reconceiving the situation, changing how you saw the whole picture.

At some point I did the sensible thing, and looked up a dictionary, because behind the knowledge there hides wisdom. The answer is, that answering is "swearing against" and it derives from fencing: sword play. My move, your retort. So problems and answers are the one dance, they summon and evoke each other. It was wise, then, to be going in search of the lyricism of an older beauty that is beyond ruthless logic.

And if answers are woven, then I am put in mind of needles wheeling like swords at play, and the image that Kahlil Gibran gave us in *The Prophet*: to get to the source of the problem, in the end one has to unweave the entire cloth. Or there is the quote from Einstein, that problems are not usually solved at the level at which we created them.

There was a certain irony in this poem now, for here I was, having bought myself a house in the country. I would never have described myself at this time as being on any kind of personal, inner quest. How I saw myself was always couched in terms of social and economic goals – looking for a means of income that was amenable to what I valued in life, looking for a job, looking for social connections or contributing to the community in some way (I was coordinating adult education programs during this time; it was very much a part-time thing, the equivalent of a few hours a week).

However, despite the low level of income that I had, I did appreciate the benefits of not having to go to a job every day. I was like one of those people who retire at sixty-five and then find there are so many good things to do that they wouldn't have time for a job anymore anyway. I had lots to do, building up my garden, making it better, fixing the house, improving the garage and workshop. And maintenance. Physically there was quite sufficient around me to engage my efforts constructively every day.

Without admitting it to myself, I can see now that I was deliberately delving into the domain of the personal, the interior. Not in the sense of a practice where I would do the same routine every day, but I would come back to it regularly. "It" involved all aspects of my life. It meant using the I Ching regularly, to put questions before it and see what it had to say, and I immersed myself in the thinking of King Wen, the man who had written the core commentary in around 1100BC, drawing on the rudimentary symbols and images that Fu Hsi had given China perhaps two thousand years earlier. And the Duke of Zhou, King Wen's son, had added to the commentary of his father, and later Confucius had studied it and added his own interpretations.

Confucius held the I Ching in the highest esteem. He said if he had another lifetime, he would spend all of it studying the I Ching. The I Ching is a conception of a world that makes sense. It is a world where yin and yang dance with each other and the ethos is created, and we are part of it, part of it all, each with our own yin-yang measure of energy. The present time, the present situation in which we find ourselves, has come on the long stream of time, events piled on events, ambitions contending with resistance, modesty sparring with ego.

The sage has understood that there are patterns in what happens, there are many patterns, but not an unlimited number, and that is why every situation that occurs can be understood in some fashion, because there is always a dynamic of forces and motivations at play within and among people. And how do we live best in this world? We live by being upright and modest, by seeking harmony with the physical world and by honouring the structures, roles and relationships of human society. We live at peace in knowing that in the world there is rise and fall, it is the natural way of things and we do not stand apart from this movement. We live best by tuning into the movement, the dynamic that is transpiring in the moment, so that we know when to run and when to stand still, when to contend and when to let go.

King Wen, for a time, sat in stillness, recalling the development of the Shang dynasty, which descended into tyranny and corruption. He realised that the life of a country, like that of a person, is a journey. I wondered what that might mean, that a country has a life in the same way that a person does, and that how a country (or a society or a culture) responds to situations determines how it proceeds and what it becomes.

I was journeying, and King Wen pronounced that the time and significance of journeying were indeed great. He describes it as a time when there is a little prosperity, not a lot, and the way to face such a time is to keep still and cling to brilliance. If you are steadfast and upright, there will be good fortune. But it is a time of journeying, so do not cling to old things and traditional ways.

There was never any question in my mind that immersing myself in the I Ching and seeking to live out of its conception of the world, its cosmic perspective, was a worthwhile enterprise. I only raise this because when I've confessed my predilection for the I Ching, some people have said, "Oh, yes, I remember dabbling with that in the early 1970s. It was quite fashionable for a time. But I could never make much sense of it. And you're still using it?" (With the inference, "Why?")

16

I was making sense of it. Murkily, perhaps, as if I were sitting on a bus and the windows were all fogged up, and I was rubbing my hand against the pane. I was getting a feeling for what was outside the window. I am more patient now. I realise the truth of what Confucius said. It may take a lifetime. Are there better things I could be doing? No, I don't find that. I have taken advice from so many people, I have tried to look at the world their way, and it's been more or less helpful, at times.

"More or less helpful, at times" is not good enough, is it? I remember, "Each our own way we must go to the desert, where the angels will minister to us". I find another poem I wrote, and I know that this is what I was doing. It related to the dreams I had as a new settler.

Yarns of the new settlers

Ten days from our boldness
and we thought that we were lost,
but we kept on moving, moving;
we did not say the things we knew
but tried rhythms, chants
and old truths.

Perhaps we should have tried harder
or not at all:

opinions differed.
Ten days turned to obscured past,
metaphysics threatened us,
politics lured.
The sky wrote it all in implacability.
Men called brothers
signed authorities for their share
in the plunder.

Once again we caught ourselves
looking at the sky;
behind, there were no signposts
to be seen.

I was trying old truths, and learning that everything was real but not everything was helpful. You have to know that this was the time that preceded the stories in *Sustenance* and *The Ten Thousand Things*. The things that occurred in those stories were things I was able to do afterwards. It was paradoxical, this so-called journeying. Apparently the only way to undertake the journey is by being still, by being in stillness. There is always that drive to be doing something, and needs that we have, and fears, so there is always enough to keep us busy, to keep us moving, moving. But the omen for the time was Mountain under Heaven – retreat and stillness.

King Wen was approving. He said there are times when it is appropriate to retreat; to retreat will be prosperous and smooth if your attention goes to being steadfast and upright. Keep inferior persons at a distance, not with ill will, but with dignity. This was a perspective I had not heard in the world around me, nor in previous circles – in society, church, school, or any other organisations. Not in hippiedom either. This was a path I was taking alone.

I did not speak openly about the I Ching. Only a few people seemed to have heard of it anyway, so I would have had to do a lot of explaining. And then I would have been slotted as someone with weird beliefs. But I didn't characterise it to myself as a set of beliefs. It was a way of seeing the world, a way of living in the world – bodily, emotionally, energetically. The best way I had found to express it was in this short verse:

Look from the place
where we are all one,
carry the light into the day,
stay open in the heart.

If I am in doubt or despondency, this is the saying that brings me back to centre. Its meaning has become richer to me over the years. Looking "from the place where are all one" is how I see the essence of ethics. (Yes, you may remember I mentioned earlier that I am currently doing a PhD in ethics.) This grew out of Albert Schweitzer's definition of ethics as having regard for the well-being of other people and society as well as our own well-being. I extend this to include the natural world as well, and hence, everything – all-that-is. So ethics is about looking "from the whole", where we are all one, instead of just considering our own (selfish) needs and desires in isolation.

The idea of "carrying the light into the day" reminds me of what Victor Frankl said about his attitude to life. To this phrase he would have said, "Yes. Don't wait for the light to come. You *are* the light. Carry it into the day." And when we accept this way of being in the world, our hearts may then be open, and King Wen adds: "Nothing is unfavourable".

It became easier to accommodate these ideas.
They took root in me. It did not mean that I had shed
my shortcomings in living in the world. I was no great
leader, or expert on anything. I was not socially
confident. I felt all the fears you might feel if you found
yourself alone in a house in a valley in a forest a long
way from a small town which was a long way from a
big town and much, much further from the big city and
you didn't have much money or a job or any other way
of obtaining an income. I wrote:

A loss of power and opportunity
(he sustains his secret powers)
I dream, dream, that's all
Lose direction
(trying, trying all the time
to hold onto the way)
Out in the darklands,
remembering, remembering the light;
is it enough to know there is a light?
And I am reeling, reeling
while I am asking these questions,
I am remembering the light
but falling all the same

What a tangle this is, the high vision alternating time
with the dark thoughts. For some, the answer is quite
simple: you should get out more. Exhaust yourself in talking
and doing, and then sleep soundly. There's some truth in
that, but it's a limited truth. You still have to come back
home, you still have to come back to yourself.

I started writing poems based on what I read in the I
Ching, writing the world from King Wen's perspective. I
called him sage.

The sage's undertakings

If others did as the sage does
their undertakings would proceed
with harmony and excellence.
The sage does not fight with circumstance,
he restrains his wrath
and banishes his fear,
ruling himself with calmness.
He takes his rest
when the mountains withhold his progress;
he moves when the obstacles clear.
In the cast of the mountain's shadow
he does not pronounce doom
but nourishes the secret hope
that hides in the heart of all perils,
retaining his clarity and resilience always.
His silhouette merges with the hills,
a play of light and shadow
dancing in the mysteries of each moment;
effortless is his force.

I wasn't writing "poems" in any literary sense. I was
writing reality, articulating the way of the sage in words that
made it make sense to me. They came easily, and with them
I entered into peace.

17

This all remained private for many years. In the
meantime, opportunities came. Opportunities to play
community roles, and exercise power in those roles. In
doing so I experienced situations that traversed the
entire vista of the I Ching – life, in sixty-four
hexagrams. I experienced the movement of one

situation into another, so that I learned how to manage transitions better and see the capacity in situations, discerning people's motivations, and looking from the whole.

In danger his only protection
is his sincerity;
with confidence he approaches the disturbance,
fulfilling what is necessary
and retreating.
When he is not in demand
he returns to his home;
if you ask him what he does there
it will not seem important.
Perhaps he watches the birds
or puts straw on his garden.
You will hear the sage in hard times —
he is sharpened by adversity.
In victory he will storm through,
flanked, it would seem,
by a dragon horde,
intent on the last crushing blow.
But at once he will turn aside,
and pick his way back silently,
knowing sadness too in that hour.
And one knows
it is only the lesser man
who would stay to mock and plunder.

If I learned anything, I learned it by wading through the ordinary stuff of each day and the incidents that came my way. I did not go looking. I wrote. I even wrote what was intended to look like a journal, something that a researcher might find years later and use to try and make sense of me. It was mischievous. I included dates and names, all concocted.

For example. I am reflecting on the demise of my relationship with my wife, four years earlier: "She was a distance away. I never got close to touching her in that time." And he surmises her journal: "He didn't care, he couldn't see I was not coping at all. Because I kept up with the washing and the housekeeping."

I even included notes for the researcher: "5th January; written in foolscap notepad, discovered among other notes and stories. Not known whether it is a biographical note or part of a story."

I wrote, also for the researcher: "The journal was different when he recommenced it eight months later. You would assume he had forgotten everything. The only thing he recorded for weeks was the number of hours he worked. He said he was recognising the importance of keeping records."

And I included cryptic notes: "For some people, this will still be a long way away (13th?)."

And there were occasional sayings that were intended to suggest great insight: "Philosophy is the study of the meaning of things. It holds the same importance today as do queues." And, "I am writing to give the philosophers something to write about, not to philosophise."

I wrote: "A journal can be so perverse that the story eludes you entirely", when what I think I meant to say was, "the truth can elude you entirely".

In one entry, I wrote about a man on a day's outing to the deep sea, fishing. The man is soaking in the warmth of the sun when he sees a fish jump out of the water. It is pale, pinkish, displaying itself in a glorious leap, then it is gone. He had not concentrated on his line all day after that. When friends ask him where he has been, he says, "I went fishing one day, that's all. I didn't catch anything but it was a nice day."

And the friend says, "So you starved that night?"

"No. I had potato soup."

And the friend says, "I've got a good recipe for potato soup."

That's where the entry ends, and I observe now: there were times when soup became important.

18

I will tell you about soup. The soup. Julie was living with me. We both said it was temporary, laughing. And it is a day when Julie is tired. She is asleep, at three o'clock in the afternoon. Her book is lying beside her, open.

Today I lit the fire in the kitchen stove. Julie usually does that, but she is asleep. She is better at it. She knows that this sort of wood does best at the beginning, and later you can add that sort of wood, and shut down the draft on the flue, just that much. But I manage.

I am making soup. It is going to feed us tonight, and it will last for tomorrow, and tomorrow, and then some more. It is made out of what is in the cupboard, and the fridge, and a selection from the field. It is called "kitchen soup".

Julie usually chops the kindling. I don't do that. She knows how to do it well. The log I brought down from the back gully seems good for kindling, and I've sawn it into short lengths. The driftwood from the creek she uses for padding, for the sitting fire that holds through the day without making a lot of heat.

There is enough kindling chopped, and I use it. With a little kerosene it starts okay. Julie sleeps; it's a cold day.

I go to the fridge. I take things out, soup things. I sort it. Some is too old, only fit for the chooks in their winter, off-season. I collect a good feed for them. The rest is vitamins and minerals, needing only a good soak and a simmer. I put on some music, all the better to simmer myself. Vitamins and minerals are called for; it is not high-protein music.

I repair to the chopping board. Julie will not wake yet. The raw smells are for me. Julie will wake to the simmering, when the vegetables are softening and the herbs have been added. But there is a zing when the skins have been excised, and the knife releases aromas. The pot fills, and I discover more than I expected in the cupboard.

It is time for the cast-iron skillet and olive oil. First you add the onions, then you allow your nose and eyes to take over. There is a capsicum, a few mushrooms. The mushrooms and carrots can be given brief exposure to the heat. But more important, my eyes scan the shelves of herbs and spices.

The pot is already on the stove, and the bubbles are rising, the water thickening. More wood; the sun is going down. Sizzle, sizzle, good, good.

Julie wakes.

"Julie, this is a big soup," I say. "It may break all our pots, or it may feed us until spring."

I have been out into the field, and the pot has stinging nettles and watercress in among the vegetables. Stinging nettle is full of iron, and it adds flavour too, and watercress is peppery and full of minerals.

"Just as well," says Julie, "I'm too cold to cook in the morning, and I never get round to it in the afternoon."

"Don't worry, I'm seeing to it. Keep the fire going." And Julie brings in more wood, banks the fire. She opens her book again, and is immersed for a while. Julie is returning from a struggle with the demons. It

71

has been a long struggle, and she needs soup for strengthening. Simple food, natural elements.

The music continues. Like the aromas, it has undertones of simple durability. Julie needs simple music, light. Anything more she treats with suspicion. Demons work that way.

The shadows draw the night in. Note that we are alone in this night, a long way from street-lights and sirens. We have lights, and we have a telephone, but the telephone does not ring.

Julie raises her head from her book. "Mmm, smells good." It was a brief revelation of lighter possibilities. I was glad. Everyone said that hope was not a luxury, but rather, an illusion. Well?

By now the soup was on its way. It had been several hours, in which time it had accumulated vegetables from the fridge, stray offerings from the field, and magic from the shelf of herbs. Sometimes, the chemistry could be wrong. But today I was not distracted; all was in right measure, and the fire had responded, had been adequate to the task. Bubble, bubble. Mmm.

In the city-world the soup would hardly merit a moment's thought. It would issue forth from a can with an attractive label and look just like a seductive advertisement.

"This is it," I said. "The soup." I announced it. "You eat it, you go to bed. And dream."

Julie felt the rise of her demons. Demons mistrust everything, soup included. But she settled down to the bowl. The night grew cold. The winter might be a respite from the heat of summer, but here at the edge of the civilised world we had not conquered cold, we struggled with it day by day. All winter we are pre-occupied, we chop wood, we go to bed early and sleep late. It saves us from more sophisticated struggles.

19

And indeed it was temporary. The demons kept up their pursuit, and Julie took herself away, in disarray. Things fall apart. There are dead spaces in time. Amid desolation, deterioration and pessimism, you can hold your values firm. Occasionally there will be small hopes, if you watch. You will see that there is an undercurrent that is pure music beneath the clash and clatter. Moments of joy, torn from the jaws of devils. But seemingly unreliable.

The question at such times is, how are you? Are you keeping your eyes pinned to the horizon? Avoiding the rampages and binges that would be easy, avoiding the need for desolate regret?

I always felt my fragility, but I always knew my strength. And into this affray a word would fall: Returning. Returning. It happens inevitably when the seasons have come to pass. I write about returning, assuredly, even when the present seems bleak and stark. Even though I do not feel the returning, I know that returning stands apart from my gloom.

Indeed, until all the seasons have played out, the door is locked. The answer is to go where you must. Alone. Against all the advice, assurances and invitations. "Come into the fold," they would say. "You are talented. We need you. There is work for you here."

I am a shepherd who turns away from rich pasture, the level plains where the sheep grow fat. Who would not want to be a shepherd here? I pack my meagre bag and walk off into the hills, perhaps looking for a stray goat with wiry flesh, or perhaps it will have golden horns.

"I am going," I say. "I will not stay here. The plains are too small." I was remembering shepherd stories, stories about terror, when a lion comes out of the wilderness and slaughters all the lambs. I was going beyond the limits of safety, but I would not be taken unawares.

The plains people say, "Don't worry about the lion. We will build a fence to protect us, we will make guns." I am not moved by the argument.

The plains people say, "You will find much hardship."

"Indeed," I reply. "I may."

I was not thinking of returning. Inevitability is for the gods. I am not a god, I thought, but I remember Jesus' words, "You shall all be as gods". Perhaps, I replied, but I am not a god yet.

I travel, further than I could have imagined at the beginning. I embrace strange philosophies, and stranger friends. I laugh and sing, I cry and I argue with these friends. I spend time alone.

There are sheep and there are shepherds. There are black sheep and stray sheep, there are lions and fence builders and sharp shooters. There are lonely places, some of them green with pasture, and there are places where you can see clearly. Nowhere is without danger.

I learn, "You can only relax when you are powerful." I laugh.

"Blasphemy," say the plains people, but they themselves are sheep, and only ever find power in their collectivity. They have their own way of perpetrating blasphemy.

Standing on a hilltop, surveying the plains, I say, "Ask the next question. What is powerful?"

I remember what has been said, that the mighty can be brought low, and when they are, then you know that their presumed power was merely a fortuitous circumstance. Temporary. Life is a moment stolen from the gods, and who lives forever?

My thoughts grow mischievous. I am not thinking of returning. Perhaps I have not fallen into sufficient ruin yet. Perhaps I am still in search of the goat with the golden horns. And I imagine a search party comes for me, to take me back. The leader pleads with me, "You know we all live forever."

And I answer, "If you say you live forever, why are you dead now?"

But there is no search party. The message I hear is, "Learn what you have to."

I sleep, knowing that it is dangerous. Down on the plains they would say, he is so poor he even has to steal a moment's rest. But I am sleeping peacefully, I have no compunction about this theft. I am obviating the need to return. I dream: "Cruel gods give way".

20

It is the ego that resists going into the pit of the self. So, into the pit I go, to that uncertainty, instability, that cauldron behind appearances. I keep the outside consistent, considered, and I am acknowledged as citizen, adult. There is some truth in that, and that is an exemplary achievement.

In the pit it is much more precarious. I sail through moments, even hours, of each day. Between, I stand aquiver, earth-quaking, darkness all around. Fearful, without hope of achieving – what? Anything "worthwhile". Or even clarity about what that means.

Of course I resist. I recognise the demon of self-pity. I shake my shoulders, turn the corner, engage in conversation, give love to strangers. And in those moments I sustain, briefly, other worlds. I feel like a television set that is turned on and turned off. In moments of engagement I am turned on, and in other moments, in the presence of the self only, I am caught, transfixed, dark, cavernous. Like the dead screen of the television when the power is off.

I read, I say the words, over and over, and if I said them to another, she would question me and perhaps she would remonstrate. She would have her own words, and I would not contest their truth. Would those words override my grey, soft-rain, held-breath cry? It's simply a tendency to be hypnotised by moments, an inherent disposition (whether genetic or environmental) to melancholy.

And sometimes I dig through that, straight through the middle of that, and am seized by joy. By the urgency and necessity of bliss. This is a feeling I have known, have carried into the fray, have used to conquer, in worldly battles.

What I know now is, I cannot rely on this as a technique. In real living there are no techniques. In ordinary life there are many techniques – nice clothes, pick-up lines, aloofness (whatever it takes) – but this is not real life. Real life operates under its own rules.

I relinquish technique, I have no textbook. I have thousands of books (which I love) and many of them are wise, but there are no rules. What is needed today is not written. The wisest book would contain one sentence: "Throw away the book." It is, and it has to be, love only, and the plunge into dark.

What is the feeling of that moment? I would say it is different for each of us, and I can only say how it is for me.

That is why I am not a philosopher or a teacher. I don't presume to formulate experience for anyone else. And if there are rules to teach, they are certainly sparse: "Meditate like this, or like that."

What I would wish is to lift the darkness, to dissolve the heaviness. I have no doubt. There is love, there is joy, such joy that you wonder if your heart will burst with it. In the quest, you may feel you are dancing with danger, but do it. It may mean coming close to another and exchanging breath and warmth and stories and insight.

21

For all my renouncing of dreams, if I did not formulate dreams of myself in the world, they came to me at night. I dreamed, love is water down the river. I stood at the edge of the exuberant flow. Donkeys and sheep floated by on the current. Then I am taken in too, and I do not struggle against the pull of the water downstream. I do not seek to interrupt it. Eventually I land on the bank, breathless. I think it is beautiful, and I breathe with all my heart.

Some of my dreams were not so benign. I had another dream, about a hero (a fiction, not a real person). The hero is an idealist from another country who speaks out against the leadership in many countries. He is visiting our country to make speeches and campaign for his causes. But I am informed that he is suddenly about to leave the country and the authorities are pursuing him. They don't like his beliefs and his causes.

I am out and about in the city, and coincidentally I see him. He is with some companions and they are driving somewhere. I follow in my car. They go into a township and into a building. I am still thinking that he is under threat and is in need of protection, so I take out my camera and follow him into the building.

He and his companions are robbing the place. I am shocked. I show myself and confront him. I ask him why he is doing this. I want to expose him. He answers me defensively (or is it defiantly?) that his opponents deserve to be robbed. They are self-satisfied and oblivious of what's important. He says that he has been clever, and he has been able to hoodwink his opponents many times, in how he got into the country, and how he got away with his actions to date.

I didn't catch what he called his actions – was it "exploits"? Did he perceive them as revenge? Was he simply taking things from them because he despised them? Were these raids, or attacks, providing resources for the cause, or were they aimed at weakening his opponents?

I left the building, devastated and disgusted, my trust ravaged. One of the hero's companions followed me out and accosted me. He wasn't about to let me get away after hearing what the hero had said. From his pocket he was getting out what I assumed was a gun, and I kicked out at him wildly.

I woke up, frantic, kicking out wildly. It took me some moments to make the transition from my dream to my surroundings. What lingered was the idea of the hero who is not what he seems. Someone I admired and sought to emulate had been a fraud, had not been an idealist at all, but a self-serving crook. I was reminded that much of my passage into adulthood had been punctuated by my discoveries, or realisations, that people I had admired were not what I thought they had been.

Caught up in the music of the sixties and seventies, I felt an accord with many rock artists who protested against the Vietnam War and seemed to stand for high ideals.

Subsequently I found many singers or writers who held up the ideals that coalesced as the counter culture. It was easy to admire them. But I soon realised that rock stars held a privileged position. They could stand on a stage and deprecate, remonstrate, rage, they could lead the chant, but they didn't have to play the tough games in the corridors of power, they didn't have to fulfil or implement ground-level change.

It was not until John and Yoko crossed a boundary in their protests that we knew that here were a couple who were serious about what they were saying (in their own weird way). Otherwise, what I saw was people with a licence to rant and no need for a day job.

The dream was a reminder that I had gone to the country, not to find another hero, but to find a new type of community where leaders were not so necessary. I was successful in one sense at least – I didn't find any new heroes.

22

I'm taking stock. I haven't forgotten that I'm here. I'm sorry to have neglected you. I have been immersed. It has been like digging up an ancient civilisation and I have been trying to put together the story in a way that makes sense to me today. And apart from various chores, there have been no interruptions. I have been digging into archives and no one has rung me to demand my attention elsewhere. In fact there was one job that cancelled on me just before I started writing. They must have known that this is more important, or at least more interesting, than what they were doing.

There was a particular poem I was looking for. I have just found it. I didn't have it typed up. I found it in one of my several exercise books that span twenty or so years, starting at age nine. This poem is written out carefully in biro, just as I'd been doing since I was a child. When I look back at all these books I have a renewed sense of amazement about computers, and how recent they are (obviously, in the sense of personal computers on which there are word-processing programs). I didn't have the facility for typing my poems into a computer until I was about thirty-eight.

The situation with the stories is different. Most of them were written during an intense period of time after I first acquired an Apple computer. This means that, although many of them were typed and saved onto discs, I have no way of getting the information off these 3.5-inch discs with their early version of formatting and software, not to mention the long-obsolete hardware.

These facts reinforce the archaeological feel of my enquiry. I am reaching across distance to find threads that are continuous – continuities. I am typing now from one of the exercise books:

Never get near the gate

Never get near the gate,
never get near the gate,
walk past a thousand times,
never get near the gate.

Never touch the light,
never touch the light,
see it only through the window,
never touch the light.

Walk on down the road,
walk on down the road,

nothing we ever did was right,
walk on down the road.

The larger shadows loom to take us.
What price oblivion?
God, father, maker of all
brick walls, barriers,
sound-proofed, multi-padlocked
secret-combination vaults,
holes in the ground,
forts and prison camps:
Who, who, who is the holy one?
I can never remember.

Never get near the gate,
never get near the gate.
What was the offer that you made us?
Never get near the gate.

This was a signature song from my city days. It was the cry of desolation for the old culture. But it was now an old song. In my sojourn in the valley I gradually disengaged from its sentiments. I melted the stone, I touched the light. The realisation of this time was about moving from discernment to forgiveness. It was good to know what it was about the mainstream, or dominant, culture that was defective and inadequate. But at a certain point you can find that you have taken on the persona of the blamer, which is the same as the whinger.

You blame both mother and father as the representatives of all that was handed down to you. But in the valley I learned the perspective of King Wen. I learned about cycles as an inherent aspect of the universe, and in particular, of human society. One of the things that King Wen did was establish an order for all the hexagrams, sixty-four of them. He began with Heaven and Earth, then he placed the rest of the hexagrams in pairs, as an insight into the unfolding of life, as a conversation between yin and yang.

You remember the jar of poisonous creatures that I mentioned? It is an image for decay, for a time when things have decayed. King Wen places this hexagram right after "Following". So he is saying, when an order is established in society, and people accept it and go along with it, they forget to question and to think for themselves. And so things become rigid and removed from their roots, tradition overtakes life, and the meaning of things is lost. Everyone is following. This is why success can be the breeding ground for failure. The jar is where the poisonous creatures gather, because no one has looked into the jar for a long time. It stands for decay.

All that outburst, when thousands protested against the Vietnam War, when music roared its rebellion, when every aspect of life was being subjected to critique, often savagely – all this was making sense to me as the natural evolution of success and following. I grew up in a society that was extremely successful at so many things, particularly manufacturing material artifacts, but it had become poor at questioning itself. But to remain in that place of blaming society, that too, would be unconstructive.

How do you start again? There was the societal aspect to the question. The answers that were offered were participative democracy, new versions of socialism, new political parties, grassroots communities, the counter culture. Then there was the personal aspect, as John Lennon had asserted ("You say you want a revolution, yeah? You better free your mind instead."). And at the personal level a revolution was occurring too, new orientations in psychology, counselling, therapy, the opening up of the West to eastern religions – The Beatles had brought the Maharishi and transcendental meditation practices into our society. There was yoga, Hare Krishnas chanting, astrology, Tarot, Reiki. Yes, the door had opened.

My question was more elemental. Instead of talking about a new label, a new "ism", a new ideology or a newly imported packaged tradition, let's ask, what does it mean to start again, at the personal level? What does it mean in terms of moment-by-moment experience, in terms of our attitudes, beliefs, values, habits, practices, ethics and behaviour?

There was a poem I had written in the early days of my move to the country. I really liked this poem. I thought it stated the essence of what I was seeking to do, whether that turned out to be in the context of an alternative community, or as a family, or my personal relationship to a local community. It wasn't until I started reflecting on all this business that I began to realise why I liked this poem so much.

I even had some copies of this poem printed, on a single foolscap sheet of yellow paper, to sell at markets. I asked a friend to do some artwork and she did a line drawing of a person kneeling in the midst of a burst of light, facing the reader, with a yin-yang symbol underneath.

Just enough

Honest the day is rising,
is quietly asking,
if there is any question
let it poke with gentle rays
into acquiescent dark.
If a rhythm is called for,
a sparkle is all that is needed
to measure the pulse
and your eyes may pound as they please.

At a touch we all discover
the secret hopes we had withheld –
discovery bathed in such great happiness,
afterwards we would call it ecstasy.
Sometimes, the earth is just soft enough
for pockets of fragility to persist
for just long enough
for us to wonder
that love is possible at all.
And then every day,
the clean face of honesty
shining for only a moment
shoots rays across the other side of space.
A day of saturation
would break you open,
split down the centre and see
if you would spill out love.

Beginning in the dark
we taste what the light would do,
hope and occasionally
stand defenceless,
tempting the fire-bright.

What is it I like about the poem? In terms of what we
are talking about, it says to me that to start again, the single
requirement is honesty. It is the first word of the poem, and
it occurs again later on. How do I describe honesty? It is to
be open to the light of what is true, and it incorporates other
ideas too. To be honest, you actually have to be humble and
trusting too. And you have to swear to yourself that you will
not dissemble, you will not cloak untoward intentions in
sophistry, you will not be glib, and you will look to see things
for what they are in themselves, and what they could be,
rather than with the blinkered eyes of those who follow their
culture unquestioningly.

The title of the poem: "Just enough" is significant too. If you realise that you are living in a culture that has lost its way and become excessive and corrupt, then starting again means to intend to be content with just enough. Interestingly, only recently a book was published that is about ethics and purpose in life and in work, and it is called *Just Enough*. Let's draw a line through time and space, from that poem written by a long-haired young hippie tucked away in the hills in Australia to the early years of the 21st century and Harvard Business School's publishing house in Massachusetts.

Can we remake the world? Yes, when we start each day with honesty, and refine our wanting to want only what is enough. After all, if we were to be split down the centre, would we spill out love?

23

It may be all very well to be honest, but what do we do about stories? Life comes to us as story, and we must make the story up. There was a story I wrote that took up the challenge.

Axil

Axil climbed upon the mountain. He looked upon the length and breadth of all that was below him. In the valley there was a fire burning. There was a man digging. And somewhere else there was a quarrel going on.

Axil had no one to advise him, and sometimes he felt it would be nice to be told what to do. But the more difficult course is not to listen to advice. So the situation was perfect in a way.

He did not give advice either. He told stories. Axil is like a man sweeping a floor, who takes time off to comfort a child, or to paint a house, or to give his love to a lady. The floor is always clean. Those who notice this, Axil calls his brothers and sisters.

On the mountain the sky was darker. The colours became confusing. Mistakes were possible in this light. Axil climbed down again, he lowered his head from the darkness to pick his way.

A stranger came, offering a torch. Axil held out his hand to take it, already grateful, when he suddenly withdrew himself. Why is it never clear? Why must he trust his feelings? The stranger was a bearer of evil, unwittingly or no, and Axil must refuse the light.

He kept on, still fearing to stumble, the torch fading and Axil's heart struggling from the attraction of its offer. Why is it never easier? The fear of falling did not leave him, but he strengthened his good resolve, and in this way distance was consumed.

When he arrived at his dwelling, the room was stark and cold. Without any reason at all he found kindling and built a fire. At the dwelling too he had a visitor.

The visitor was glad to see a fire, and was warmed by it. Axil offered tea, and they talked about essential business. Eventually the visitor went away, and Axil was not quite sure why the visitor had come. There was so much Axil did not understand.

In the morning the fire was out, the log half-burned, as if it had stopped the moment Axil fell asleep.

Axil was not sure whether things happened anymore. The morning was calm, in a cyclical fashion: the mornings always seemed to be calm. Axil tried to think what had happened since the last calm morning. But the kookaburras laughed at him, even the swallows whistled sweet nonsense.

Axil thought, "Ah, the morning is refusing to answer," and was amused. He decided, "Perhaps the morning is in the possession of a sweet and gentle goddess, and the evenings belong to a demon."

Again he thought, "I didn't ask to be in this game." He started to look for a safe place, so he could sit and watch the game. In the game there was a doorway marked "Marriage" with a coloured glass panel.

He was handed a number of cards, which he began to read: "The green glass is for companionship." "The yellow glass is for bliss." "The blue glass is for two people working together."

He walked through the door. There were no instructions about this, but the door did not resist him. He looked around, and thought to himself, "It seems comfortable in here."

He looked at the next card. It said, "It is possible to be comfortable in this room."

In one corner a girl sat with her back to him, suggesting unhappiness. He said, "I would like to talk to you."

She said, "What do you want?"

He said, "Nothing."

She said, "Can I see your cards?"

He showed her. The cards said, "The door has closed behind you. It will take violence to re-open it." And the next: "Assume that this person does not understand you."

She showed him this card. "What do you want?" she said.

"To see you happy," he said.

"What would you do to make me happy?" she asked.

"Nothing," he said. "There is nothing I can do."

The lady trembled, then burst into tears. "You are very selfish," she said, and tore up the cards to throw at him.

Axil walked slowly to the door. It took no violence to open it, for the lady had already overpowered it in the anger and haste of her departure. The yellow glass for bliss was scattered with the other colours in fragments on the floor.

Outside the door, Axil was handed other cards. In despair he saw that the demon-time was approaching again. "Does anything happen?" he asked, "Or is this another cycle?"

It was necessary to read the cards: "These cards are about answers." "For one answer you must look. Seek everywhere, with all your senses keened." "For this answer you must dig. Dig until you know you have finished digging." "This answer you must construct. There will be sufficient instructions, although not very many. You must think." "There is another answer which you must keep alive. Learn how, quickly." "Another answer, also, needs to be preserved. It is perfect to begin with; you do not need to do anything to complete it."

Axil looked for more cards. Again the failing light confused him, and he looked with suspicion at the little man who had appeared.

"What do you want?" he said.

Of course, the little man wanted to see the cards. "There are too many answers here," said Axil. "Too many answers is as bad as having none."

The little man read the cards and said, "These are not answers, they are just stories."

Axil moaned.

"Ah," said the little man, "you must exorcise that demon." And having said that, he disappeared.

"More advice?" wondered Axil. He lit his fire, but could not sleep. He had a visitor. Female. She was intelligent, meaning one who can see within things, who can distinguish between things. He told her about the stories.

"Who makes up the stories?" she asked.

Axil shrugged, "It depends whether it's morning or evening."

"Rubbish," she answered. "That's just when you read them." Axil had no answer to this.

"Let me tell you a story," Axil's visitor went on. "I hope you don't mind. It's a story about the night.

> Gerard pointed out a particular star to his companion.
> 'You see that star?' he said. 'I have a rope tied around that star, and when the time is right, I will draw it back to me.'
> Sophie was intrigued by such a claim, but she wanted to test Gerard. 'What sort of rope is it?' she asked. 'Is it made of wire, or thread, or nylon?'
> 'None of these,' answered Gerard.
> 'What, then?' asked Sophie.
> 'The rope is made of love,' answered Gerard.
> 'You laugh at me,' rebuked Sophie.
> 'No,' replied Gerard. 'In love I have let this star chart its own course. And out of love one day this star will steer its course back to me. This is true.'"

Axil pondered this story. At last he said, "I will tell you one of my own. There was a ship which was painted blue, and it sailed off into the ocean, where it encountered a storm. It sank. There was also another ship, which was white, and it sailed off into the ocean, and tore its hull open on a reef, and sank. What does it matter that one ship was blue, and the other one white?"

"Tell me what the little man said," answered the visitor.

"He told me to exorcise the demon," said Axil.

"Well, then," said the lady. "We paint the ship yellow, and it refuses to sink. "

After that the visitor and Axil went to bed. The fire continued to burn while they made love, and then while they slept.

In the morning Axil said, "The love refuses to die. I have cast ropes around the stars."

The visitor said, "Remember," as she left.

In the afternoon the little man came by and said, "The ship is sinking."

Axil smiled and said, "Is blue or white?" And because Axil refused to look at him, the little man disappeared.

24

Then again, it is just a bit presumptuous to say that we make the story up. Yes, we do, and then again, it's also true that the story has to accord with the nature of the world. It has to make sense of us in the cosmos, as physical beings with consciousness. I went to a concert, and an aboriginal girl sang and talked. She talked about the Mother, Mother as earth, as the spirit of the earth that sustains us all. She said she had lost herself in city ways, technology and aspirations, and then she found herself again – she came home to the Mother.

This was in the city. This was now. In a suburban hall where the crowd was a meeting of generations, and of people from both city and country. Time has passed, and you can imagine a scenario where a cohort of new settlers found a rhythm and persisted, and aged with their long hair growing greyer over the years. And you might wonder whether they descended into routines that worked but made them indistinguishable from others, a parallel stream among members of bowling clubs and sports clubs, church parishioners and the Country Women's Association.

But you might wonder, too, if there were some who found a faith in those early days, and had seen a purpose and had continued to live from that place. Not the property where they had built their first shelter, not the land where they had planted their first garden, but the place of oneness with the Mother.

I listen to the rhythm of drums, and in the dark of the hall a man tells a story about creation. It began with souls before there was anything, and they careened in bliss. Then there was love among the stars, and things began to take shape. The focus came down to the soul that knew it would be born, and the agreement it made with the sky, to remember the oneness.

And then the soul is born into the world, our world, as flesh. And there is a moment at which the soul forgets all, forgets everything, and that is the moment of birth. The drums continue to beat out their rhythm, for there is a second agreement, and this is, that in living our lives we will look to remember where it was that we came from.

It was one of the godfathers of the early new settler years who was speaking, who had lived a few kilometres over the hills from my valley. Someone I had not known. He was speaking poems, long stories in rhyme about the early days when the rainforest was being logged and a group formed to fight it through direct action, going into the forests and standing up against loggers and chainsaws, bulldozers and logging trucks, unarmed but with a passion for the necessity of what they were doing. Afterwards, when the laws had been passed to preserve the forests, they discovered that their action was unprecedented anywhere in the world.

Afterwards, as well, they discovered that someone, a professor in Norway, had developed thinking that articulated what it was that had inspired them to act to save the forests. The professor called it "deep ecology", and described it as a philosophy that recognises the inherent worth of beings other than humans, which is to say that other species of life, as well as rocks and mountains and oceans, have value in themselves, not merely as resources for us to use, and use up. Because there is mystery in how life is sustained, and the least we know is that it seems that all life is interdependent, existing in self-sustaining ecosystems.

It's strange, said the godfather. We found that we belonged to a global community, us at the end of civilisation, living in rough shelters in valleys and forests at the end of roads, meditating and living with just enough. No, he didn't say exactly those words. But I can, for him and for me.

25

I went to a Book Fair. It's a continuing conversation, my story and the world of "out there", and it's symbiotic. I walked into this crowded hall, amassed with books, and my experience was magnetic. Within five minutes a dozen books had summoned themselves into my bag. "I am relevant," said one. "I contain gems," said another. "I will turn your head sideways", said a third.

I have become better at this. I don't waste time. I operate efficiently. Once my bag filled, and that happened remarkably quickly, I went to the checkout. All done, at $27. Then I visited a friend, had a conversation where I surprised myself again with what I said (I only learn through speaking and writing), and went home.

Cup of tea, and spread out the books. Keep a notepad, a pencil and some bookmarkers handy, and wade in. And wow! There is even a comment on what I am doing. In a book called "Way of Zen", there is a poem from Tung-Shan, a 9th century Chinese Ch'an master, who says: "Do not seek the truth from others. Go your own way entirely alone. Now there is no way that you cannot meet it. It is everywhere."

I get the paradox, the cosmic joke that I am reading this in someone else's book. But I am gathering what is meaningful to me, not handing my life to an alien set of instructions. And the universe moves in time. The intimations are everywhere. Every book I pick up informs my quest.

We all notice this magnetism. But in our society we are inclined to reject its significance and joke (uncomfortably) about it. We say we are imagining things and advise ourselves not to be gullible. But what if we took a different stance? What if we just accepted it and said "Thank you"? What if we went even further, and adopted this as a strength? Walk in surrender to your purpose, and the flowers will fall all around you like an Indian wedding.

What makes your heart warm? That is the question. This is it: at sundown, in late spring and long after the sun has bowed out, but before the ascendancy of darkness, the crickets twitter and the cicadas drone. On and on, and my heart falls into its richness. And the more I fall gladly, the louder they declaim. The kookaburra comes over the top of it, raucous with the laughter of knowledge and insight. Huh!

And I read, this time from David Hawkins' *Power Versus Force*: "We don't dance from logic, we dance from feeling patterns. We make our choices from

93

values, and values are associated with intrinsic patterns." And the kookaburras think that is good for another laugh. I know, from day to day, that they are enjoying my investigations and articulations.

Now Jung wants to get in on the act, and say something about mythology, which is another counterpoint to logic (from Robert Segal's book, *Jung on Mythology*): "For all his insistence on the inner, psychological function of myth, Jung maintains that myth also serves to connect humans to the external world." Segal says this is how life becomes meaningful. The world that was impersonal becomes invested with responsive, divine personalities. You have to slow down and take those words one at a time: responsive, divine, personalities. Ah, it is grand. This could be a good life.

In a way, it is already complete. Beyond this point there are projects, possibilities, experience and the development of expertise. The requirement is just to say "yes" to the patterns of purpose in the universe, to keep saying "yes" to the positive – peace, joy, honesty, acceptance, strength, compassion. As it became in my house in the valley – the months passed, and the surface of the pond grew still, until my resolve grew clear. I became present.

John O'Donohue tells me (from *Eternal Echoes*): "A tree is a perfect presence. A life that wishes to honour its own possibility has to learn how to integrate the suffering of dark and bleak times into a dignity of presence." I had a tree near my house that was my spirit tree. A eucalypt (*Eucalyptus grandis*, I think). I kept an eye on it. It grew right next to the stream in a gully, surrounded by smaller trees and undergrowth. From the house you could not see the trunk, just the branches and crown rising over the edge of the gully.

I guess it was about eighty or a hundred years old. When the first farmers came here, they started by building a shed nearby, about fifty metres further down the stream, and they lived in that for some years before they built the house up on a small prow. A wise move, because in flood times, the water rushing down the gully must have come rather close to their shed. When they arrived in the valley, the tree would have been young, maybe twenty years old. Its crown at that time would still have looked down on the shed. Perhaps it shuddered as all the trees around it were cut down to make pasture for the dairy cows. But they left this tree as a shade tree for the cows.

Trees observe all this. They see like a tower, and incorporate all that happens around them in their trunk, their branches, their leaves. They soak it in while standing tall. Their leaves are shed like tears and laughter, and their trunk grows ever more solid. In high wind, their branches exalt as they bend. They bow and you know they are not being beaten, they are weathering and withstanding. When the rain falls they make the sound of glistening and forgiveness.

Thus my spirit tree stood, and grew, imperceptibly, whatever was happening in the world. I needed to learn only this much.

26

There is learning through thinking, and there is learning through doing. I learned this in Herman Hesse's *The Glass Bead Game*. Magister Ludi Joseph Knecht, the intellectual at the centre of the book, is at one point involved in a discussion of the relationship between thought and history, and he comments, "Abstractions are fine, but I think people also have to breathe air and eat bread."

Just so, the time came for me to go out and take on a project. I saw myself in contrast, or rather, contradistinction, to the godfather of activism I described above. My way, I resolved, was not to broadcast a new ideological platform, but to create something that would speak for itself. I would articulate a minimum set of principles and follow their logic. I would only articulate things if it became necessary. I did not divulge much at all about myself, my background or my sources, except as it became relevant to the purpose at hand. I never, for example, mentioned the I Ching.

When I started the job as manager of a disability services organisation, the president put around a notice that said I had two degrees. I didn't; I'd started two degrees, and dropped out of both of them before completion. I finished teachers' college and had been a teacher. What would have been more to the point to mention was my experience as a psychiatric nurse, and my encounters with people with disabilities in the environment of a psychiatric centre. It was apparent to me at the outset that honesty needed to be a core operating principle in this organisation.

The central importance of honesty was reinforced just a week later when the president was arrested for embezzling all of the organisation's funds. It was quite an introduction to the role of management for me. It became clear that I needed to quickly develop some other qualities too – leadership, so that people would not lose heart, and authorities would trust me enough to give us some money to keep going. I needed basic management competencies with finances, staff and administration, and a positive vision so that there was a reason for everyone to remain and build something better.

It was a sudden immersion. If I'd asked for a practical project where I could live out the principles I had been developing in my mind and in seclusion, I certainly got it.

The great irony was that in the first week the president told me to take my time, learn the ropes slowly and get used to the people and the ways of the disability sector. Yet he was the reason that I had to get competent and capable at speed. But when you are ready, in an instant everything can be transformed.

Who knows what value was ultimately served by this work? I told the story of it in *The Ten Thousand Things*, from the perspective of ethics and leadership, and the insights offered me by King Wen and the I Ching. Was this "project" an appropriate pathway for me to take as a way of re-engaging with the society I had withdrawn from? And was the way I did it appropriate?

I wasn't "in my element" as a protester, although I was comfortable as a rebel. The long hair made its statement and marked me as someone who did not subscribe to the whole package of societal membership. In "coming back", it also meant I had to work hard. It was as if the bargain was this: okay, so you're obviously a bit different, and I suppose you think you've got something decent to offer, that might even be better than what we're currently running with. But let's give it a go. We'll give you some time and we'll pay you, and you show us that your way works.

I was thrown into a burning circle, to dance with the lion. If you read my account of the journey (in *The Ten Thousand Things*), perhaps you will see this. I think that if I had started by laying out my philosophy, I wouldn't have lasted long. No one in the organisation wanted a philosophy, they wanted someone to show them that things could work when you operated with decency and dignity. King Wen says, "The revolution is only believed in after it has been achieved."

The central principle I expressed through the organisation was that our purpose was to enable people with disabilities to live in dignity and to develop and exercise their capacities as far as possible. The real operating principles were left for the most part implicit. It was implicit that I would operate with honesty and openness, given the legacy of the former president's embezzlement. It was implicit that I would lead by serving the best interests of the people we provided services to, and their parents, and the staff, and that I expected staff to do likewise.

And – I'm only articulating this now – I felt that it was more powerful that way. We approached principles through behaviour. If a staff member left someone sitting on the toilet for half an hour I asked why. I tried to do it in a way that kept the principles as the attractive thing. Mostly I let the principles fill the space unspoken.

Over time it became more evident that we were all learning to allow our behaviour to rise to fulfil the principles, and there was joy in this endeavour, for all of us. Staff came to work with expectation, that maybe Marty would learn how to do that task today, and to enjoy Helen being more independent in herself.

There were forces of darkness at play in that story, and eventually it became necessary for them to destroy what we were doing. They gathered together, compatriots in their need for suppression, harshness, control, and opportunities for corruption. The curtain came down for me. I don't want to give away the story, because the story takes some telling, and it's in *The Ten Thousand Things*.

I'm looking at it now as the project of an "ex-hippie" for whom it was a means of re-engaging with society. For a time I saw it as a failure. I didn't think I had done so badly myself. I had indeed learned to be competent as a manager and as a leader. Of course, you could well argue, if that's so, then why didn't you use your supposed skills to sort the problems out? Isn't it the very definition of a good manager that it is one who succeeds?

It went over and over in my mind: they smashed everything I built up over six years. Then: I've got nothing to show for six years' work. I was shut out; few people would talk to me apart from neighbours in the valley. For some of them, my whole commitment to the job had been misconceived anyway, when I had a house, a property and a garden, and I could be at home enjoying it all. But at a deep level, I knew there had been value in what I had done, and I didn't have to feel responsible for how it ended up. There were larger forces than I understood at the time which determined the outcome.

My job now was to learn what I could from the experience. It had been an experiment in creating an environment where work and business could be carried out with integrity, ethics, creativity and joy. It was another way of making these values manifest in the world. It didn't have to be a separate, self-sufficient society; in fact, it was the idea of self-sufficiency that was the real mistake. I had figured that out soon enough in my first year in the valley.

We all subscribed to the doctrine of self-sufficiency: grow it or make it yourself or don't use it. That first year in the valley, I thought my way through the implications of this, item by item. The previous owners had been good examples. They had dairy cows and they only sold the cream. After the skim milk was separated from the cream, the skim milk flowed down the hill in a pipe (no pump needed) to the pig shed. The pigs were fattened up on skim milk plus corn that the farmer grew himself. And they grew most of their own vegetables. A nice little eco-system.

However, the logic had to be applied selectively. He still bought building materials. There were still foodstuffs that they bought, such as flour. But I was still thinking it through. They bought flour – well, you could grow wheat, and have your own hand-grinder. You could grow beans for protein. Et cetera, et cetera. It eventually came to this: what about cooking oil? Well, you could grow sunflowers or olives, and grind the seeds or olives to produce your own oil.

At this point I started to feel that the whole quest was misconceived. If you did all these things you would be enslaved to a panoply of year-long, wasteful and inefficient processes. If you were actually successful at all of these things, you would have an excess which you would be wanting to sell, but no one would want any of it because they would be doing the same thing at their house. It seemed to me that I was working against human history in order to achieve a goal that would make everyone isolated from each other.

It was best to go back and ask why I had started out on this path. What had been the impetus to want to leave the city and live self-sufficiently? What was the perceived evil I was rejecting, and what was the value of the ideal? Okay, I remember. It was dissatisfaction with being isolated from nature and natural cycles, and awareness that this had happened to the whole of society. If everything that happens has some constructive value, then the value of the hippie "experiment" was that it brought everyone's attention to this disconnection.

Well, even if not that, at the least, it brought my attention to it. And perhaps the quest was still purposeful. As William Blake said, "One does not know what enough is until one has understood what constitutes excess" (or something like that). What was unchanged was the goal of living with awareness of nature. Well, it had changed, but only to become clearer. I would express it now a little differently, more nuanced. I would say, aware of being in nature, being part of it. And I would want to be clear that this awareness was available to someone living in an apartment building, on the first floor with no view of the mountains or forests or the ocean, not just to someone with a house in the hills and their own garden outside.

Then I had to combine this aspect with what I had experienced in the organisation about working with people. Years later I articulated this by saying there are four domains in which we live. Other thinkers have approached it differently. Howard Gardner, the "multiple intelligences" man, says there are several different types of intelligence, for example, logical, intrapersonal, and natural (appreciating nature). I look at it this way: we live in four domains. One of them is the natural world, one of them is your own body/mind, one of them is the interpersonal (people you know and interact with), and one of them is society.

It turns out that Ken Wilber (he of integral psychology) says something quite similar, in his four quadrants, but I didn't know about that when I made up the four domains. Is this just like the hippie activist and the professor of deep ecology? Perhaps it makes me part of a global family.

The kookaburras in the grove of gum trees next door think this is a great laugh.

27

I have this to say to those who plotted and carried out my destruction: you never broke me. What I gave, I gave freely. What was lost was not essential. I went home and took all my clothes off and dived into the creek. The dirt washed off and I came up clean and cool. The casuarinas bowed over me with gentle fronds.

I sat still for a long time, shedding, letting go. Everything I learned I kept.

I read and wrote for four years after that, finally getting a degree, in business. I was a nomad, as John O'Donohue says, journeying from threshold to threshold, and another dimension of my soul was unfolding.

In the short term, it seemed that I had lost, that the thugs and crooks had done their work and what I had built, in spirit and in flesh, had proven inadequate. Yet all of those people who had been in on the kill, lusting for my blood, all of them seemed to disappear over the next couple of years – left town, don't know what became of him; left town, isn't missed at all; left town, is rumoured to be living in obscurity somewhere.

When I studied for my business degree I was looking for signs of the same spirit in the business world that I had sought to create in my management job, the spirit I was exploring with King Wen. King Wen had a complete picture of the wise leader, that he reveals bit by bit through the images in the hexagrams. He threw light on events of the moment, and he shed light on the past. He said, "When the Shang tyrant is overthrown, you inherit the care of the people", and he made me think of those first days after the president was arrested. Yes, that was what I knew at the time: I knew that I had "inherited the care of the people". It was knowing that that made it possible, nay, necessary, for me to continue.

What King Wen said to me about going back to university (and I realise, this is another instance of "going back") was expressed in the image of the tower, from which you look down on things: at first yours was a quest for personal identity; now it must become a quest to create a new way for people to live and work together and in harmony with the earth. I was recreating a pathway, going back to the beginning, unmaking wrongs, remaking. I was weaving answers, this time. When I was in danger of believing in my defeat, King Wen summoned Ming I to comment, and I wrote this in thanks:

Ming I: Darkening of the Light

Ming I sees the wheel of his life,
clouds steer over the mountain,
as dark as a pit,
but the eternity of his actions
is in the issue of his sincerity:
the light of day is in his love.

Darkness fails to rule —
the proud prince falls in confusion
at his moment of triumph;
the land stirs again:
emptiness awaiting the light.

Ming I turns into the darkness, pure,
empty of false hopes;
he clings to joy like flame to wood:
it is the nature of evil to pass.

28

I came to the idea of focusing on ethics in management in my business degree. In all the management-related units I studied, I looked for this aspect, for what writers had to say about it, and whether it even arose as a pertinent issue. The treatment was generally apologetic, as if to say, well, we've got to say something about this. The approach oscillated between "good citizen" rules of thumb, like the Rotary Four-Way Test, and potted versions of the major theories in moral philosophy.

The Rotary Four-Way Test, I thought, was intuitively appealing. It seemed to address all the aspects that most good citizens would want an ethics test to address: Is it the TRUTH? Is it FAIR to all concerned? Will it build GOODWILL and BETTER FRIENDSHIPS? Will it be BENEFICIAL to all concerned?

At the intuitive level, other writers added the exposure test: if your decision or action turned up on the front page of tomorrow's paper, would you want to have acted differently? And there was also the Legal Minimum Test: Is your proposed action legal?

I couldn't see that there was any attempt to reconcile these intuitive tests with the discussions of ethical theories. It seemed there was a high road, where you argued about ethical theories in the company of Kant, Hume, Aristotle, Mill, Bentham and the like, and a low road, which had a pastoral aura and which tended to suggest a rather quaint, slightly holy and ultimately parochial stance towards business conduct. Both of these approaches were doomed to be bowled over by the brash steamroller of business.

It seemed that university courses were in awe of the juggernaut of business – it was not be criticised. The absurd and repugnant dictum of Milton Friedman in the early 1960s, that the only responsibility of business is to maximise its profits, may not have been shouted so loudly as it once was, but it still underpinned every conversation about business, it still drove every business course. To question it was to prove yourself squeamish. So, nothing had changed since I left the city, and mainstream society, and went bush.

I enjoyed learning about current business issues and business thinking, the theories about management, and the laws and practices of the business world. There was a lot to read and think about. I could have chosen to request entry into an MBA course rather than enrol in a Bachelor degree. I had twenty years' experience covering numerous occupations and including six years in an executive management role, as well as four years' university study behind me. But I was starting over, and I wanted to do it right from the start. The appropriate thing, in my mind, was to start at the beginning, and no one would be able to say I had missed steps.

I made one exception. Psychology was at that time a compulsory First Year subject, and I had completed Psychology I in one of my lapsed degrees twenty years ago. It had been a gruelling immersion in behaviourism – supposed insight into human life through the behaviour of rats. I had a look at the current syllabus and decided the current course wasn't going to enlighten me much further, so I examined the "Advanced Standing" option. Could I get an exemption?

The rule was, the course had to have been completed within the previous nine years, and you had to provide both a transcript of your results and a course outline. I had a transcript of my results, but I didn't have a course outline, and I was eleven years late. But I decided I wasn't going to be beaten by this. What I did find when I went searching through my filing cabinet was a whole folder of notes and assignments from the course. I still had it, after twenty years. Pathetic? Let's see.

I took my transcript and the folder of notes and assignments, about 50 pages in all, handwritten notes, typed assignments with tutors' marks, into the Psychology lecturer's office. I told him the course I was doing, and asked him for an exemption. In short, he took a day to look through the notes (or not, I don't know) and he granted me the exemption. I picked up the notes, took them home, and ceremonially burnt them. I figured they had now served their purpose. I had carried them everywhere with me when I left the city, and they had sat in a filing cabinet in my house in the valley for years, waiting for their moment of justification.

I chose human resources management as my major. After my management experience I was interested in the human side of organisations, what motivated people and what it took to lead people well. But ethics sat at the centre of my focus. I also had a conviction that these two things – ethics and management – were integrally related, in the sense that you couldn't be a good manager unless you were committed to operating ethically and with integrity. And it was clear right from the start that ethics was a topic of great discomfort in the business environment.

I completed the three years of the Bachelor degree, and then it was easy to decide to stay on for another year and do the Honours year. I had some work casual teaching at a local high school, so I was getting enough money to survive. When it came time for me to choose a topic for my Honours work, I decided I would ask human resources (HR) staff what their views were on a number of ethics issues. The university leaned strongly towards empirical studies rather than dissertations and qualitative studies, so I thought I would make it easier for myself at this stage, and follow that line.

I conducted the survey with the help of the professional HR institute, who let me distribute the questionnaire at a conference. I obtained enough responses to make the exercise worthwhile, and I learned enough statistics to do a creditable analysis of the data. What I would say about my findings is this: when I asked HR people specifically about ethics, they recognised what ethical issues were, and could identify some (in fact, quite a few) ethical issues that might arise in their organisation. But when I asked about their views on a range of ethical issues, their answers were frequently inconsistent. It indicated that they didn't have a considered view on ethics, they just responded ad hoc when an issue arose.

I completed my thesis, received my Honours degree and some praise, and left in search of a job. All this time, while I had been studying, I had been considering this moment. What would I do when I finished my degree? There was no chance of my getting a job in the district. I had tried that after I got the sack, and no one was interested in employing me. Potential employers readily believed that I was innocent and competent, but what would "others" think if they employed me? I was a hot potato, and they didn't want to handle me.

Leave the valley and go back to the city: that was the proposition. I wanted to work in a job, I wanted to have that kind of engagement with society, and the only future if I stayed in the valley was an ad hoc life of casual teaching, which would be to waste the promise of what I'd been doing for the last four years. How did I feel about the prospect of going back to the city? (And I included the option of getting a job in a regional centre rather than the Big City.)

I took a while to think about it, in fact I thought about it as a likelihood the whole time I was studying. Eventually I became reconciled to it; I thought it would be okay. In the valley, I loved waking in the morning and hearing the cry of the birds echoing up from the gully. That's how it seemed, cries echoing up from the gully, but I felt that this was permanently in my heart now, and would be no matter where I was in the world.

What was this feeling? It was that here, I felt loved. It must be like the aboriginal woman said, coming home to her Mother, the earth.

I hadn't realised, until now, the right words to say it, but this is it: there, I felt loved, I was at home with my Mother, the earth. When I heard that creek flow, just down from the house, it flowed out of the deep heart of the earth, it was the ghost river of King Wen, streaming omens from the source of wisdom in the mountains, and the hills around me were where the spirits expressed the movements of heaven and earth, all the phases of the I Ching from beginning to after completion.

It was time to go, but I would not be leaving in spirit. I shed no tears when I packed the furniture, took piles of rubbish to the tip, mowed the lawn for the last time and checked the still-growing garden. I organised the removalist, packed the car and drove away, down that rough dirt road to the bitumen road, then onto the main road, through the town and eventually to the highway that went all the way to the Big City.

29

I live in the city

I live in the city,
but at night I hear
the sound of the mopoke,
and in the morning the laugh
of kookaburras.

I live in the city,
but it is an abode.
I sojourn here.

I wonder about the people
who see it like a prison,
their eyes focused on a tiny square
of barred light,
hoping for Noah's dove
to bring them a branch
of olive
from some paradise
buttressed by remoteness.

I live in the city.
I admit that at night I hear
the sound of traffic and trains also.
But there is silence in between,
and it is the same silence.
I ask,
is it the traffic that is silent,
or the mopoke?
I burn a candle.
The flame is steady.
The flame burns
oxygen and travail equally.
Travail withers in the still burn
of wick in night's embrace.
It is the same light.

30

    I became a writer and commentator on "industry". I got to the city on the strength of my writing skills, to a job where I wrote articles and commentary on human resources, training and development, employment law and management. And ethics. I reported on professional events, seminars and conferences, and I had licence, time and resources to research topics in all of my designated areas. I wrote commentary that was soundly based on research, but also helpful to practice; it wasn't just "theory". I was using my experience in management.

I was also, in my mind, serving my apprenticeship in writing. Not that I was under a master or mentor, but I learned from my colleagues about tone, the appropriate stance to take, the right level of detail, and how to structure topics from the top down, and then how to construct good paragraphs and sentences. I learned not to be precious about my work, but to revise and edit, to take it apart and reorganise it so that it was more amenable to the reader. I became a good self-critic, or at least, a better one than I had been.

Admittedly, the publisher I worked for was seized for a while by gung-ho forces who thought all life was marketing, and who had no head or stomach for substance (that is, what we were actually writing that was of value to our subscribers). But substance won out in the end (as it had to do), and we all learned something from the marketers, even if grudgingly. Life might not be all marketing, but it is always a conversation – there is always an audience, even if it is implicit (as it is for me at this moment). There is always a listener who might have his/her own views and insights, and who is best served by our clarity and empathy.

For a while I had to write commentary for a payroll product, which was right outside my domain of expertise or interest. But I learned I could do that too. I had other products to draw material from, so I didn't have to make it all up from a blank page, and there was a given logic to it, so I approached it methodically and delivered what was required. And it reinforced the craft aspect of what I was doing in this place. I was refining the craft of writing for particular professional, and practical, audiences.

110

I learned, too, why people don't like to write. To write is a choice and a commitment. I don't mean in general; I mean every sentence, every word. To explain something or tell a story you have to commit words to a page (or a screen) in a certain way. There are millions of ways to do that, even for a one-page story, but most of them are clumsy, irrelevant, annoying, confusing or just not very effective. Some people sweat when they have to write down a story or an account of something that happened. Every word reveals a stance, or it can distort what you want to say. Words can be very recalcitrant. Think of a lawyer in court cross-examining you, taking your words apart and deriving a completely different meaning from them, and parading this in front of the judge or jury. That is the power and the peril of words.

But I didn't want to be a writer who is seduced by his own words. My motive in writing is either to explain, or to summon the wind, like Walt Whitman. For a few years I edited a training magazine, and many times I wrote articles based on interviews with professional people. They could talk well, but they couldn't have done the same if they'd had to write it themselves. Many times I would send the article to the person and they would respond, "It sounds better than I did." Smile. Yes, that's what I do. Not "better"; simply a more fluent, coherent and lucid version of what you said.

In one hexagram, King Wen says, "Work through joyous words to bring spirit to expression."

31

In writing about all aspects of professional practice for trainers, human resources practitioners and managers I was able to consider, again and again, the part that ethics plays in work. In one respect it was a fringe issue. In a large-scale survey that the human resources institute conducted of its members, where members had the opportunity to identify the five key issues that faced them as they looked to the future, dozens of issues were identified, from industrial relations to management development programs and the use of technology. But ethics wasn't mentioned at all, nor anything that could be construed as a proxy for ethics.

Yet, as my survey had shown, if you specifically asked the question about ethical issues, then they had no trouble identifying many areas that at least needed keeping an eye on. So ethics occupies a curious position in the mind of people at work. It's there in the room, but if the overt topic of attention is business-related, it doesn't get mentioned. I am thinking, what does this mean? In one respect, you could say it is about how business is defined. Business is defined in a way that excludes the relevance of ethics. It is an activity that in our current society denies the jurisdiction of ethical constraints – and it is permitted to maintain this stance.

The way back into the business world for ethics has been the concept of social responsibility. This seems to have occurred, in lumbering fashion, through the widespread impact of a number of corporate movements, fads and phenomena. The era of "downsizing" was one, where ruthless executives radically reshaped their businesses and their means of production, and slashed their workforces to such an extreme extent that, in the US, whole towns were devastated. The executives, of course, at the same time that they were annihilating the livelihoods of thousands, were paid huge bonuses.

There was an essential obscenity about this conduct, both in terms of the cavalier disregard for the well-being of society, and the greed and selfishness of the executives, that gave rise to the idea of the social contract. (I am not trying to be a textbook here; I am trying to follow a thought in order to throw light on what it is I am seeking to do in my own work of writing about ethics.) The realisation was that these corporations were so big they could actually affect the whole of society, so the rules had to be changed.

My analogy is littering. If one or two people throw their personal rubbish at the side of the road, it's undesirable, but it doesn't affect the whole of society very much. (It would if everyone acted in this way. That's another issue.) But when a large company, which is using public infrastructure and making huge profits for shareholders and giving huge remuneration packages to its executives, dumps thousands of tons of poison into a river and kills all the fish, it's a problem that governments need to address. The company's conduct is having an impact on the whole of society and the governing bodies of that society have to be responsible for the well-being of society by reining in such companies.

Next thought: this doesn't mean that the conduct of the one or two people who throw small quantities of litter on the roadside is not blameworthy. I think that the way the process goes is that we often ignore small problems because they are small, but when we have to face a big problem of the same nature, when we've dealt with that, we go back and address the small problem, applying the same principles. But if we think about what the main issues are in the public mind, that loose gathering of unexamined talk and opinion that "does the rounds", like a virtual version of talkback radio, then the idea of a social contract is associated primarily with big companies.

The implication is that you have to be socially responsible if you are a company that is big enough to affect the whole of society (in an obvious way). But, if you are not so big, then you can probably stay below the radar, and not pay too much attention to ethical constraints. Of course, you need to pretend that you care, but this is just good public relations.

But my real interest was not in the interplay at the executive and government level, where power bumps up against power and both sides are attempting to win public opinion. My interest was in the people I talked to frequently, the people who had roles further down the corporate pyramid. What was their experience? Well, I already had some indication of that. They carried on with business in a way that didn't acknowledge the relevance of ethics, but if you asked them explicitly if their work posed ethical issues, they could readily give you a list. And my question was shaping up: can we do better than this?

32

Part of the problem is the conformism that being employed by an organisation engenders. There was a book written in the 1950s, *The Organization Man* by William Whyte, that examined this phenomenon. His insight was to see how modern man was being subsumed into large-scale bureaucratic structures dominated by a functionalist climate that thrived on its own logic of operation. This was a climate in which the question of human purpose was displaced by the never-ending quest for better technique, which is exactly what Jacques Ellul had argued. In a sane world, purpose would be the driver of innovation; now we had a situation where technique was becoming its own raison-d'être.

Whyte was the editor of *Fortune* magazine in the US. I was a child at the time, but I suppose these ideas diffuse into the ether and can end up in the minds of schoolboys in a far-off land. I described my feelings about the organisation in my early twenties – my resistance to its insidious lure.

A roundabout trip

It's a roundabout trip,
learning to walk
two yards to mother's arms,
learning to talk in syllogisms,
acting in accordance with form.

I have known people
with springs and gear-wheels
inside their heads,
too many people,
people after the roundabout trip:

I-am-a-nine-to-five-man,
I-have-a-pretty-wife,
and-a-house,-car,-and-two-children.
Good-morning.
Good-evening.

I have seen the junk
accumulate around me
and I am crying out,
telling myself while I am still alive:
not here, not here, not here.

We have been so long in the dark
that even beauty is frightening.
Direction-blind we watch any spark
that could lead to our enlightening,
wanting to be strung out towards the mark,
and to see the distance tightening.

Let me not worship false gods.

In a dull climate like this, people's sensitivities are suppressed. Thinking and personal decision-making are overtaken by rules and scripts, so the scope for being ethical is just about eliminated. Responsibility (which is the essence of ethics) is pushed off to a safe distance. Then along came Milton Friedman with his dictum about the responsibility of business being to maximise profit, so the responsibility for ethics got pushed away altogether. It's up to the government to substantiate ethics in the form of laws.

One of the things that is really contemptible about Friedman's dictum is that in denying any ethical constraints on business, it actually appropriates the language of ethics to do so. The word "responsibility" embodies the essence of ethics, but he is using it to turn ethics away, by claiming there is a moral obligation to maximise profit at the cost of everything and everyone else. What I find truly amazing about this stance is the extent to which it was just accepted. As I've noted, to this day it still underpins most conversations about business.

All that needs to be said about Milton Friedman's dictum is that it is an ambit claim. The absurdity of our society is that it took this ambit claim at face value, as if it were pronouncing a great truth about life. But it is no different from the child who says (in a very bold voice), "I should have all the lollies." The point about an ambit claim is that it is preposterous, and you don't really expect the other person to believe you, but wouldn't it be fantastic if they did?

But, to give a simplistic account of it, society did swallow Friedman's claim, and doesn't that begin to explain the obscenity of much corporate behaviour, and executive behaviour, since then? When US companies like Enron and Worldcom and Tyco fell apart, and HIH and One.Tel in

116

Australia, and governments decided that perhaps it was time to prosecute a few executives, didn't they all act as if they'd been caught with their hands in the lolly jar? Oops. But then, of course, they tried to justify themselves – they didn't take very much, they deserved what they took, they really did a lot of good, indeed, they were brilliant.

In the same way, companies put their hands in the lolly jar of society, taking what they can get away with. The trouble is, because everyone is involved in the share market, either directly or through a superannuation fund, we are all said to have a stake in the lollies too. Any dirt is on our hands too.

However, I think this is a questionable argument and not a central one. I think it is simply used to divert attention from the real matters of substance.

If we do what society should have done in the 1960s and reject the marginalisation of ethics from business, maybe we can formulate a conception of business that serves humanity, in contrast to the prevailing concept that being in business means having a licence to plunder. Then perhaps I wouldn't have had to escape to the bush in the 1970s, to leave the wasteland that had been created by profit obsession and the vacuous quest for improved technique.

The signature fable for our times is "The Emperor's new clothes". The sobering thing about this tale is in the very title – in fact, there are no new clothes. The central obsession of the Emperor, the novelty of the new, spins off into a fantasy that becomes ever more dissociated from reality. And the courtiers and the couturiers are both the desperate authors of deceit and the victims, caught in a lie of their own making.

What would it take for things to be different? In fact, not much. Just one thing, to stand the world on its head. I think we have all suffered from a simple delusion. Think of life as consisting of two circles, Big Circle and Little Circle. The little circle is inside the big circle; it is a subset of the larger set, like "hammer" is a subset of "tools". Now think of business and society. What we've been fooled into thinking by the folks in business is that the Big Circle is business, and society is some small subset of that.

This is the delusion. The reality is, there is no business without a society, and in fact, there is a great deal of society that lies outside of business, like watching the sky or hugging a baby or singing a song. The truth is, the Big Circle is society, and business is a Little Circle inside it. We've just got it back to front, and it suits certain people who live inside the business world to have us believe that business is the Big Circle.

What's the effect? It poisons everything. It poisons human relationships. It infects watching the sky and hugging babies and singing songs. It infests us with a disease that has two symptoms: (1) it invests the activity with the objective of profit, and (2) it distorts the activity so that the focus becomes efficiency (technique).

I'm willing to concede now that my rejection of society was extreme. Here's a funny example. It was just after we had moved to the valley (the "we" is an historical reference to Meredith, my wife of the time, and our two young girls). I was committed to hand tools. I was not going to use machines or power tools, anything that required fuel or electricity. We had a slow combustion stove which we used for all our cooking, so we needed an ongoing supply of firewood. I used to scavenge logs from wherever I could find them around the property and cut them up small enough to use in the stove.

Meredith's parents came to visit. Her father was a good photographer. He used to develop his own black-and-white photographs. So there I was sawing up this log into smaller lengths, with a bush saw. The wood was old and dry, and it was hard work. He came to watch me and laughed uproariously. Why? Because right next to me was an enormous circular saw blade, still mounted on its spindle on a wooden stand.

Remember I said that the previous owner was very largely self-sufficient? Part of his set-up was a small timber mill, where he could saw up his own logs. The engine was gone, the wooden frame for the table was mostly gone and the rest was rotting, but the blade still sat there, rusty and disused. And there I was next to it, sweating over a hand saw to cut up logs for the kitchen. My father-in-law said, "Just let me get a photo of this. There's irony here."

I have to say, he was not being at all malicious. He just saw the irony. After he got home he made a large print of this photo and sent it to me, as something to think about. After a while, I went and bought a chainsaw. I was slowly making my way back into society from that moment on. I guess Meredith would say, "Not fast enough", or, "What did you gain, anyway? All that, to find out you were wrong?"

But, that was then, this is now. Who's to say what is a long time or what is necessary? I think it was all necessary.

33

The Big Circle is society. Not business. So when the bold boy says, "I should have all the lollies", the parent says, "No, you can't. We will make some rules that are for the good of all". This message is not unprecedented. Amidst all the rampant posturing of business people in the 1960s, Peter Drucker had stated the proper place of business. He said – in *The*

Practice of Management in 1955 – "The purpose of business is the creation of a customer who sees value in what the business offers. The function of profit is to validate the activities of the enterprise and enable it to continue."

This is as good a formulation of the proper purpose of business as you are ever likely to read. This statement has been sitting there, all this time, when business has been going crazy with greed and power. Drucker's statement locates business appropriately as a Little Circle inside the Big Circle. What could we say about ethics now that we have things in proper perspective?

Ethics is contained, simply, in what the parent above just said. It just means, what is for the good, or the well-being, of all. If you want to fill out the meaning of this, think of the four domains: the natural world, your own body/mind, the interpersonal (people you know and interact with), and society as a whole. You can consider particular aspects of life – physical, financial, emotional, cultural and so on. And you can ponder the conflicts that sometimes arise between this aspect and that aspect. But when it comes to self versus others, or self versus society, ethics asks, what is for the well-being of the whole?

Albert Schweitzer articulated a definition of ethics very much like this in a speech he made in Paris in 1952. He said, "In a general sense, ethics is the name we give to our concern for good behaviour. We feel an obligation to consider, not only our own personal well-being, but also that of others, and society as a whole".

Next step: If this principle is something we want to apply to society as a whole, then it applies to everything inside the Big Circle, that is, it applies to business. Now we have a principle that humanises business, because business, as with everything else inside the Big Circle, needs to serve the whole. If people within the business sphere seek to subvert the goals of business for greedy and destructive ends, society can call it back to its proper place. It can tell it that it has stepped outside of its legitimacy.

Objection: The objection always raised to this scenario is that we all rely on business to produce the goods we use. "Business" produces our food, our houses, our furniture, our transport and our amusement. Think of the little boy again. Think "ambit claim". Yes, "business" makes things, but it is society that determines the nature of the licence under which businesses operate, and it knows when it is being stood over. It is society that has to judge when a party is not serving the well-being of all and when it is taking too much from other parties, or from society as a whole. Parents don't let children run the show or abuse each other.

34

It seems that when I want to focus on the experience of individuals in their work lives, and ask what their understanding of ethics is, and what their experience of ethics is in the workplace, I have to say something about the big picture: what are your assumptions about the place of business in society? What is your world view?

I wrote this statement when I was putting together my PhD proposal:

Many people, if asked to tell the story of their endeavour to work ethically, would tell a story about being subjected to workplace environments where standards of human decency are lacking. Their stories would be about disappointment, in leaders who would have them think there is no point in trying to live an ethical life, because life is a struggle for survival and domination, where you take what you can get for as long as you can get away with it. This is a great sadness, and it calls for healing.

There is the ghost of William Whyte in this statement. In it we see people who, as employees, belong to the organisation, who depend on it, and who trust it to enable them to exercise their skills, develop their capabilities and do so in a way that honours the dignity of others, both colleagues and customers (or clients). It implies a faith, which we might call a naïve faith, in the willingness, indeed, the commitment, of leaders to be decent.

But the prevailing myth is that the world is tough, and that business is a game for the strong. I have been in situations where this has been said to me, as a justification for managers pressuring employees to do things that are at the edge of what is actually a shared sense of ethics. For example, a company wasn't meeting its ambitious sales targets, and it was getting close to the end of the year. So there was a decision made to send expensive new products out to a mailing list (existing customers and prospects), together with an invoice.

Of course, the recipients weren't legally obliged to purchase the products; they were unsolicited. They could send them back. But that put the onus on the customer to take action and deal with the mailing, and getting the invoice cancelled. The view was that the company was bound to get a good percentage of sales out of this "initiative". What is curious about this situation is that the sense of the ethics involved is actually shared. The proposers of this initiative know they are treading on dubious ground, because they feel a need to justify their actions. The arguments that the

122

objectors put up are pushed aside, yes, but the proposers know exactly what the objectors are saying.

So, what gets said by the proposers? "Business is a game for the strong." "Fortune favours the bold." But of course, subordinates (let's use that language) never get the chance to question this mythology; it is simply presented as a truth about the world. And if the subordinate doesn't like it, the subordinate knows what the subordinate can do about it. There is no room for an alternative view to even be suggested.

Ah, who wants to be having this conversation? It seems so futile. And what never gets said in these one-sided conversations is how much money the executive walked away with as a bonus. This is the real game, the one that is being played with the employees.

The word "intractable" springs to mind. There is an entire life cycle embedded in this little scenario. The executive has got to where he (or she) is by demonstrating that he subscribes to the myth. He has shown that he is strong, which is to say, he can do what needs to be done to win, and he can prevent any instances of insubordination from arising. He can be cruel if need be, and charming on demand. He doesn't mind being hated, because the car he drives is so much flashier than what ordinary people can afford.

This executive goes from failure to failure unscathed, because he always moves in companies that are big enough to absorb his failures. These companies survive on momentum and mythology. What they seem to need at the top is a cohort who can keep the masses performing adequately, but at the same time prevent any threat to the longevity of the cohort itself. This is achieved through a process of careful selection. The primary requirement is that you subscribe to the belief in the necessity of and the

123

superiority of the cohort, and that you can integrate with the cohort socially.

In the less palatable manifestations of these cohorts, the executives' behaviour can become sufficiently excessive or self-destructive that the whole organisation is put at risk. The lavish lifestyle of the Enron executives is a good example of this. Drug use is another common problem, particularly cocaine.

The great irony of this common corporate culture is that it occurs in societies that describe themselves as democracies. It would be difficult to think of something less democratic than the structure and functioning of a corporation. But have you ever heard anyone observe that this is an irony? When I studied human resources management, and management theory, we discussed communication, consultation, participative decision-making and merit-based promotion, but in the "real world" things seldom work this way.

I think that, in the best organisations, there is an implicit pact between the leader and the workforce (the people). They do not operate as a democracy, either structurally or as a process, but this is not what really matters. What really matters is trust, and this is how I would describe the substance of that trust: the people trust that the leader has their well-being at heart. Everything else assembles itself harmoniously around this pact.

It is a miracle that this ever happens, because the prevailing myth is still Friedman's dictum. We might call it Friedman's curse. A little circle has usurped its place in the great scheme of things.

35

It is a miracle that what I call good leadership ever happens. How could it, when the recruitment process for leadership is so heavily geared towards preserving the existing lifestyle and beliefs of the prevailing leadership culture? When I was selected as the manager for the disability services organisation, I was a default choice, because it was a country town and there was hardly anybody who put their hand up for the job.

So the recruitment process was not significant. What was significant was the memo that the president circulated in the first week, saying I had two degrees. He knew it was a lie. It was a test, to see if I would collude in the lie. If I did, I would have shown myself ready to be complicit, worthy to "join the club". I was saved by the fact that before I could even decide what to do about this memo, he was arrested. Subsequently he was found guilty of embezzlement and he went to jail.

What this meant was, I was the only one standing. The committee was in shock (and who knew who knew what, and whether any of them were involved in the embezzlement too and were lying low in case they were found out). I stood up, and persuaded the government department to give us some money to keep the services going. After that, I had a great deal of autonomy, so I had the opportunity to shape the organisation the way I wanted. It was my great experiment in whether it was possible to run an organisation with integrity.

My experience was, it wasn't simple; there were always temptations to be less than honest. In addition, there were also situations where I had to weave a course through a number of complexities, and the only way I could decide what was "ethical" was in terms of the bigger picture – what was for the well-being of all, all things considered. Sometimes, I wouldn't have wanted all my decisions, or all of my reasons, out on public display, but my actions were never determined by selfishness, and always by my considered assessment of what was for the well-being of all.

Years later, I read Joseph Badaracco's book, *Leading Quietly*, and felt recognised. I wasn't alone in my desire to lead ethically, or in my understanding of the subtleties and difficulties of doing so. The people who say being ethical in a leadership position is simple – it's just a question of having a clear and strict set of rules – cannot have actually experienced it themselves. There are always multiple values and interests at play, and you have to find a balance among them, and that's not even the right word. Balance doesn't always give you the answer either.

It is only in the imagery of King Wen's commentary on the I Ching that I have found some measure of confidence in approaching leadership. And it is not an answer, it is not a method, it is not a technique. It's this: in absorbing the images and thinking, I become more perceptive about what is at stake, and I become more perceptive about the human and physical dynamics at play. This is capacity-building by being still. Self disappears and I become the universe, I become the desire for the well-being of all-that-is.

In one place, the image King Wen offers is a green shoot, pushing up through the earth. At another time, he offers the image of a tree on a mountain – it is a harsh environment, and if the tree is to grow strong, it must take its time and put down strong roots. And in another place, there is a well, the source of pure water, and while the position of the village may change over time, the position of the well does not; we need to remember this – the nature of the source of life does not change.

The best that I can do is to imbibe all of these images and the stories around them, and get to understand the underlying truths about the world, and people, and the spirit within it all. Does this seem too tame for the strong men of business? I would say, remember that the sage is not timid:

> You will hear the sage in hard times —
> he is sharpened by adversity.
> In victory he will storm through,
> flanked, it would seem,
> by a dragon horde,
> intent on the last crushing blow.

King Wen tells us that yang is Heaven and yin is Earth, yang is the Initiating and yin is Receptive, and both are needed. It is yin and yang together that make the whole. You need both, and you need to know when the situation requires the Initiating and when it requires the Receptive. And even the Receptive is not passive. King Wen talks about yin as the docility of the mare and says, "gentle and docile, when it is put in motion it is strong and firm". Too much yin: soft, weak, lacking in spirit; but too much yang: hard, brittle, not enough elasticity.

This is a poem I wrote about following in the path of King Wen:

The old men have a saying

> They read from old books
> but do not worship time;
> caution they observe
> in all their acts.
> Who is inspired by their docility?

Soldiers, gypsies or timid men?

Not the timid —
these men know when to move
with flash and fire,
when the right touch will loosen
the spirit's desire;
in crying, laughing,
in silence and in speech
they cling to their inner strength.

What is it they teach
from their old books?
Correctness, and beauty.
The old men have a saying:
Love the One.

And I say: the truth is quite different from what the prevailing leaders have been telling us. They have been free-riding on the impetus of history. In fact, they are serial failures. The best indication of this (apart from the recurrent financial crises we experience, and the waves of corporate failures)? The complete lack of correlation between executive salaries and corporate financial performance. Enough studies have shown that movements in executive salary simply do not correlate with movements in their companies' financial performance.

When the company's performance goes down, the executive gets a salary increase because his (her) job is really tough. When the company's performance goes up, the executive gets an increase because he (she) deserves to share in the rewards. Or the executive's salary goes up because there is another company somewhere whose executive gets paid more than he does. Or the executive's pay has to be increased because that's what you have to pay if you want to get the best.

The truth is quite different. The prevailing myths have to go. Myths can be true, as embodiments of deep truths about the nature of the world, its essence, its spirit. They can also be convenient rationales, fictions concocted by the powerful to perpetuate their position.

36

Today's news: there has been another instance of executive deceit threatening the life of a large corporation. This one is Japanese, but pick a country, it could be anywhere. In this instance, the executives falsified the accounts over many years to cover up bad investments. The affair came to light through an employee who eventually became a whistleblower.

His story is the usual whistleblower's story. He tried to raise the matter internally, and the executives did everything to shut him up. They ignored him, then they punished him by transferring him, and they cut him off from contact with colleagues. They isolated and ostracised him. He was painted as the troublemaker, as delusional, as being himself dishonest. Now his face is on the news and he is telling his side of the story. (But he will get no reward.)

The extent of the financial losses is not yet clear, but the effect of the scandal on the company's stock price was immediately catastrophic. The company is a world-renown brand, known for quality and innovation in its products. It could go down, and quickly, like the Arthur Andersen accounting firm did in the wake of the Enron collapse. For Arthur Andersen, the writing on the wall was seen very quickly – it could not survive as a company once its integrity as a firm of accountants

129

was exposed as a sham, and its demise happened in only a few weeks.

Will the Japanese company go the same way? If it does, it will join dozens of others around the world that have gone this way just in the last couple of years. And its story is unexceptional. It follows all the same patterns of executive behaviour in such instances. And the critical statement from the whistleblower? He said the executives acted as if they were not accountable to anyone; they were a law unto themselves. When he expressed dissent, their response was single-minded – to crush him. There was not room for the employee to be heard, to give a contrary opinion, or express any doubts.

My perspective on this? I look at it from the perspective of Friedman's dictum: there is only one goal of organisations, and that is to make a profit. So of course it is to be expected that executives would try to cover up a financial loss, a failure. I am not saying that all executives do this, or even most of them, I am simply saying that the temptation to do so must be immense. There is only one goal, and if you are failing to achieve that goal, what do you do?

I say, a company is more likely to achieve financial success when it realises that it has to have a broader focus, beyond one goal. It is unbalanced and ultimately self-defeating to focus on the single goal of profit. Drucker pointed the way. In his description of the purpose of business, you can see a whole system at work, an ecology where numerous aspects are recognised in relationship with one another, and they are held in an appropriate balance that happens to be sustainable.

This is the picture that is given to us in the I Ching by King Wen, grounded in the initial eight trigrams of Fu Hsi, which are constructed on the foundation of yin and yang. I want to explain how yin and yang underpin life and, accordingly, business as well. Yin and yang explain why it is unhealthy to pursue a single goal. Does this seem crazy? Surely it is goal-setting that has enabled such progress and success in our society? There is a whole coaching industry that is dedicated to helping people to formulate goals and devise action plans to achieve those goals. And the core of this effort is the idea of the single goal that drives you. Isn't "having a goal" what it's all about?

Accordingly to yin-and-yang, no, it isn't. What's wrong with the single goal? The yin-and-yang perspective says that there is always another goal that needs to sit with the first goal. It is between them that a whole is created, not one on its own. It is this false paradigm of the single goal that has misshaped our society and most of its endeavours. It is this faulty mental model that delivers us so many business people who act unethically.

This is how the idea of yin and yang applies to the business context. Let's say a person has a desire to start a business. Suppose he has invented a camera, and he has a vision about people everywhere using his camera, and appreciating how terrific it is. He will be hugely successful. And we think that's all there is to it. All he has to do is devise an action plan to bring his vision to fruition. But from the yin-and-yang perspective, that is not all. He also has to know *in what manner* he will pursue his goal. In other words, he has to know his ethical values.

Think of successful entrepreneurs who are widely considered in society to be admirable. What do we say about such people? We say two things – we admire them because they were able to fulfil a great vision and make it successful, and we find them admirable as a good person. We would not admire them if they were a crook or a thug. Their moral principles are integral to their success. I say, we tend to separate these two things, the business goal and the commitment to ethics, to see them as accidental associates, but they are integrally connected, like yin and yang.

But....there are people who are successful who don't seem to be very ethical. I say, well, there are also plants that grow in poor soil, but if you were setting out to plan a garden, would you plant your seedlings in poor soil or healthy soil? Or would you base your rules about gardening on the renegade plant that does well? Exceptions need careful scrutiny.

To take another example. Consider a swimmer whose goal is to win an Olympic gold medal. Isn't this a single goal? Well, yes it is, but the ethics are still implied. This person could choose to pursue the medal by looking for supplies of steroids that are undetectable. Or, they could do what we assume and expect, which is that they will pursue their goal with honest, intelligent and dedicated effort. The yang is the goal that is spoken, but the yin, the ethical principles, is always present, even if silently, in the admirable winner.

In the yin and yang symbol, the two parts make up the full circle, the completeness. The yin and yang elements are in dynamic tension. They are not opposites, like weak and strong; they are two aspects that are complementary to one another. This is what western thinking is not used to. We think that there is goal-directedness and its opposite – lack of direction. And yes, that is a dimension, but we fail to see there is a complementary dimension, or aspect, that is needed as well – in this case, ethics or moral principles. And the ethics may also be strong or weak. In the successful entrepreneurs that we all admire, both the striving and the ethics are present and both are strong.

Another example I like is the yin-and-yang of power and grace. Gymnastics illustrates this well. Admirable

132

gymnasts are not simply strong. Rather, they combine the qualities of power and gracefulness – two different aspects that complement each other to make the whole. Either one without the other will not do. Watch the gymnast, and you see the harmony of power and grace.

The yin-and-yang principle also makes new sense of another phenomenon. It has become a joke in management conversations that a thinker or consultant will have a model of their thinking that is illustrated by four quadrants. This goes right back to the 1940s when Blake and Mouton presented the Managerial Grid. On one dimension was attention to Task, and on the other dimension was attention to People. You could be high or low in each dimension and hence we get a range of different management styles.

When we look at this from a yin-and-yang perspective, it makes sense. People and Task are the yin and the yang of the management role. All those debates about the virtue of being high in People skills or high in Task skills are debates about the functioning of yin and yang in the management role. And what the yin-and-yang perspective says is, the healthiest situation is when both yin and yang are strong, and they are held in a healthy balance, a dynamic tension, with one another. People and Task are not opposites or choices, they are both essential elements of the one whole.

I would venture to guess that any quadrant representation in a management context is actually dealing with a particular yin-yang whole. Each dimension is necessary, and each is complementary to the other. Each needs to be strong, and kept in balance with the other.

From the yin-yang perspective, we can no longer see ethics as something extra, or optional. It is an integral part of the whole; there is no whole without it. The faulty thinking of our society, that tries to ignore or marginalise ethics, just as it ignores art, music and feeling, makes us ill. We are cutting off part of ourselves. The ethics, the art, the music, the feelings, are not add-ons, they are part of the whole. At the very heart of our business, they must be.

When you look at a yin-yang symbol, in many versions you will see a dot in the middle of each of the yin and the yang parts. This is to say that yin lies in the very heart of yang, and yang lies in the very heart of yin. You see, the mystery gets deeper. It is not even as if we are trying to make room for yin as well as yang. Ultimately we come to see that yin lives, and must live, in the very heart of yang, and vice versa.

If we consider again how Peter Drucker described business and management, it's not so hard to see the dots. There is purpose and there is profit. In business, purpose must live in the heart of profit, and profit must live in the heart of purpose.

37

At this point, the master-of-the-universe manager gets impatient. He says this is mere philosophy. It doesn't help in making decisions, the tough decisions, that real managers must make all the time, every day. And I say, we create the world that we live in. I'm suggesting that the world the master-of-the-universe manager has created for himself/herself is inaccurate, and it is killing both him/her and all of us.

I suggest that the tough-guy manager stops, let's say, just for a moment, and looks around, at interesting things. Here's an interesting thing. Jack Canfield and Mark Victor Hansen had the idea that people might like to read uplifting stories about the goodness of people, and they began making a collection of such stories. They called it *Chicken*

Soup for the Soul. It sold millions, and now they have turned it into a series, looking at specific topics (parents, golfers, you name it).

Tough guy says, "Well that's just silly, and it's a display of weakness. It just celebrates weakness. If it wasn't for tough guys like me, the important stuff in society wouldn't get done. Society needs me."

Okay. Next thing: storytelling has been used extensively by leaders throughout history, and, more to the point, there has been a recent increase in attention given to the relationship between storytelling and effective leadership. What? A connection between storytelling and effective leadership?

Tough guy says, "How could that be? Oh, I get it. They must be stories about heroism, about great leaders who show how tough they are."

Well, that's one kind of story, true. Stephen Denning, who had been an executive at the World Bank and who discovered the importance and power of stories, says that stories can be told to communicate who you are, to spark action, to convey values, to communicate the personality of the company (branding), to tame the grapevine (settling rumours), to share knowledge, to foster collaboration and to lead people into the future.

Tough guy says, "Well, I tell my people a story. I tell them it's tough out there and they need to shape up."

Here is where Denning points out that most companies do not perform very well over any length of time. They are unable to sustain growth, their record on successfully adopting innovations is really poor (less than 10%), and the success of mergers and acquisitions, a favourite corporate strategy these days, is similarly abysmal. Another thing that's interesting is that managers commonly pride themselves on their adherence to an evidence-based approach, they love measurement and proof. Yet faced with evidence like these facts, they continue to do the same things.

What managers would normally look for at a time like this, that is, responding to their poor performance record, is a new technique. Denning doesn't offer a new gadget or technique. He says that managers need a new discipline, and it is one that is invisible to conventional management thinking – "because it is at odds with its fundamental assumptions".

Tough guy says, "Stop this nonsense. My time is valuable."

Denning persists. He reminds us that to this point, corporations can't claim to be so successful. Many companies survive on momentum, but they don't shine. Most of them are afflicted with failures in their business initiatives, they are especially poor in their ability to institute changes, and morale languishes at chronically low levels. So listen, tough guy, is your record so good? Or do you just measure it by the size of your remuneration package?

What's the message of *Chicken Soup for the Soul*? The message is, it spoke to people's hearts.

Tough guy says, "That's okay for down time, but I don't want my employees wasting my time at work on this touchy-feely stuff."

What's the message of *Chicken Soup for the Soul*? The message is, the employees of all these tough guys give them 10% of what they've got to give. The bare minimum. So that's all the tough guy has got to work with to make his company a success. Is it any surprise that companies perform so poorly? We are inclined to think that companies generally perform much better than they do.

Consider Enron. For years, everyone thought that it was performing spectacularly well. Then it crashed with debts of over $US35 billion and everyone was upset. Lots of people (especially employees who lost entitlements) lost money. But who goes back and revises all their previous impressions of Enron's success? No one. Somehow, all those false impressions remain unscathed, even though they've been contradicted by the later evidence.

If you go back, what you have to do is take the $US35 billion loss and spread it across, say, the previous ten years of the company's announced earnings for each year. Not so pretty, is it? Each year you would have been saying, not "Wow, fantastic!" but "What's going on? This is a company in deep trouble." Year after year: "What's wrong with the management? Why isn't someone doing something about this? And why are these managers getting paid obscene amounts of money and wallowing in luxury?"

But we don't seem to do this. All those false impressions of success somehow seem to stand unscathed, despite the contradictions. And we think it is over, the bad guys have been found out, and we'll clean up the damage. We don't think about it still happening, in lots of other companies, now, where the executives preen themselves and crush anyone who expresses doubts or, perhaps, suggests that the financial figures are not what they seem. And the tough guys keep talking about their heroism.

What's the message of *Chicken Soup for the Soul*? In Denning's book about storytelling, he has this quote at the start of the first chapter: "Storytelling is fundamental to the human search for meaning". The tough guy thinks he's got a story, but it's only a story for himself, in which he is the hero. But we know that the further managers ascend the pyramid of power, the more they are likely to become insulated from reality, and from genuine feedback. We have the accounts of the last days of Enron and HIH to show us this. The leaders become more and more bombastic and less

137

tolerant of dissenting voices, even when the dissenting voices are not even expressing an opinion, but just relaying sober facts.

The message of the Chicken Soup books, and of Stephen Denning, is that there has to be a story in which the employees have meaning too. And when we see that we have a meaningful part in the company's story, then we are liberated, we can come alive, and use our energy and efforts, our intelligence, our problem-solving skills, and our care for the customer.

38

Here's another story. It would make a good Chicken Soup story. There was a flood. There were great rains, sudden downpours that swept away cars and roads, bridges and houses, and several lives. Then the waters accumulated in the rivers, and descended on the city, flooding hundreds of streets and thousands of houses. It was the worst flood the city had experienced for forty years, and many people were in trouble. People were staying in community halls; some were cut off from their families.

And there was a telephone company, a large commercial player. Their people saw what was happening, and it was all happening rapidly. They thought about what they could do to help, to respond to people's immediate needs. They saw that communication was important. The problem was that some of their mobile phone towers had been knocked out of operation by the flood waters, there were people who had lost their phones in the wet, and there were people who didn't have mobile phones.

They decided to do a number of things, and to do them as fast as they possibly could. They transported portable mobile phone towers into the area from hundreds of kilometres away. They had to survey the city area and quickly find locations for these towers that would service the area, and get vehicles to those locations. This would mean that mobile phones would work, even across areas that were inundated.

They also offered free mobile phones to people affected by the floods, with free credit for three months, so people could communicate with each other and let them know they were okay, or if they needed something. And this was implemented within a couple of days, with staff on the ground offering the phones and helping people to use them. There was no obligation on people to become customers afterwards.

I don't want to make too much of this. It is a big company and it could afford it, and it probably won them new customers for the long term. All of what they did made good business sense, but there were two distinguishing features. First, they didn't do what many companies do, that is, immediately go and spend twice as much money on the advertising campaign that tells people how wonderful the company has been. I found out because I know an employee of the company. This initiative was communicated internally so that staff knew what the company was doing.

The other feature of the story was this. In telling me the story, the employee was moved, so proud that the company he worked for thought about what people needed in this crisis, and then put things into operation as rapidly as the need called for, with a generous spirit. Everyone worked together to deliver the help. At times like this, he felt that he worked for a company that had a heart, that was aware of human need and was willing to respond.

It's not weak to have a heart, and in fact, when you recognise that you have a heart, and so do the people who work for you, then you come alive, and so do they.

It's life and death that wakes us up. I read in a management book about a manager who worked hard and suffered all the stresses that managers do, and then he had a heart attack. He didn't die, but he faced death. He encountered it and it gave him a different perspective on his working life – he developed a different sense of what was important. But that is not what really changed him. He had some time off work and then came back. And nobody talked about it. The conversation, as before, was only about work things, goals, targets, tasks, production problems. Nobody talked to him about his experience or his feelings, or gave him the opportunity to do so.

This was what really changed his outlook. His personal experience of nearly dying and what it meant to him was an undiscussable in the work environment. It had no place to be heard. It was at this point that he realised how sick his work environment was, and he decided to leave. He had to go somewhere else and find a place that recognised that we are all humans first, before we are managers and professionals, salespeople and technicians. He could see that being human was the Big Circle, and in his work environment, being human was treated as a very little circle.

My moment was when I was in hospital after a motor cycle accident. I was there for many weeks, having a series of operations and slowly mending. I was twenty-three. I was in a big, general surgical ward, and I saw lots of people in all stages of medical crises. One afternoon the nurses wheeled in a new patient on a stretcher. There was an air of seriousness about it all, and the doctor came, the nurses fiddled with a lot of equipment – tubes, monitors – and eventually left.

I was immobile, with skin grafts underway, swathed in bandages and leg in plaster, so it wasn't even an option to think about visiting. But he was a long way away anyway. I don't think he was even in his body. As the night came on, and the bustle and clutter of dinner ended, it was silent. I believe I caught a glimpse of his eyes, frightened. I had a sense of him high above his bed, clinging to the ceiling and looking down at himself. I knew in an instant that he would die tonight, in the early hours of the morning. You will have noticed, although I have not said it, that he was alone. I lay in my bed and wrote this poem.

At the edge of the shadows
(for Mr B)

The grey man is heaving up his last breaths,
long after exhaustion,
getting dragged further into the shadows.
In the morning perhaps he will lie
dead like a sack against a back-alley garbage bin.

And I'm sorry, man,
I'm not going with you.
The crumpled photos in your pocket
are of lost days, dead, gone,
and the photos in my head
are of good days yet to come,
days that will ignite
with joy, and love, and children.

Is this what your eyes are straining at?
Old man, your flesh is already cold.
You lean on me, yes,
and I will remember your eyes,
but my way leads through happiness.
And when your eyes find me again,

141

at the edge of the shadows,
I swear I will have found a way,
something more than crumpled photos.

I have always realised there is a disturbing mix of emotions in these lines, and that some may think I am being harsh towards Mr B. But I was confronted and confused, and I could do no more for him than to be with him in dying in this meagre way, and look for hope. And I say, all our actions must countenance death. Perhaps the business world is so unsatisfactory because it is an escapist plot. It is an investment in a fantasy of power that ignores our essential mortality and vulnerability.

The angle that Stephen Covey (you know, *The Seven Habits of Highly Successful People*) uses with respect to this topic is "No one says, on his death bed, 'I wish I'd spent more time at the office'". I wouldn't put it quite that way. I think this is disparaging of business, implying that a genuine, life-respecting form of it is not possible. What I would say is, "All our actions must countenance death", but, on your death bed, you could be quite happy that you'd spent all that time at the office IF you had been working with a full heart, and honouring the humanity of those around you, and working for a worthwhile (human) purpose.

39

I wonder about my coming back to the city. I remember my house beside the creek, I remember the sound of running water, the constant bubbling, that I could hear even inside the kitchen when it had been raining a lot and the water was up. I remember swimming in the creek the day after a flood.

The flood had been so strong that all the weeds had been scraped off the bottom of the creek bed, and I could see bare sand and sandstone. The water was a translucent green, and was still running strongly. And it was cold, so much colder than usual. Days before it had been warm, sluggish, and when I walked it stirred up mud.

This green vibrant water, pouring down out of the mountain, the ghost river, it was the kind of water that tingled the skin, and when I emerged I felt so alive. I didn't have to think about whether anyone liked me, or whether I was a success. It was as if all the casuarinas above and surrounding me bowed down their limbs and fronds and said, "Now you know."

When I started in my job, the one that brought me back to the city, people heard where I had come from and said to me, "What are you doing here? Why did you come back? What you had is what half of us dream of being able to do. We want to escape."

I understood what they were saying, and I understood why what I was doing seemed crazy. All I said was, "I'm living my life backwards." And I thought it was better this way. I'd already had my "freedom", if that's how you depict it, so I wasn't hankering for it. I was content to be paid to write, that is, to learn how to write competently, and be able to speak to an audience. What I was writing about was how to be a competent and ethical professional or manager. It was a privilege, not just a job. I didn't know if anyone read what I had to say, but I wrote it anyway.

And why shouldn't I write what I think? I'd actually had several years of experience in a management role, some of it turbulent and torrid. On top of that I had an Honours degree in business. I'd done my homework. But what I was really bringing was the voice of my heart, I was speaking to the ache inside the heart of the business world.

Someone asked me the other day what I would say if I was suddenly on a stage with the chance to speak to a young audience, people who were coming into their work life with an open mind but great misgivings about the nature of the world they were in. I said, "You have to know that you are okay. Before you do anything, before you prove anything about your excellence or your competency or your uniqueness, before you go out to perform great feats, you have to know, deep in your heart, that you are okay. In the eyes of the universe, as you are, you are accepted, and loved."

Perhaps all I am is a watcher. Perhaps all I can do is listen to sublime music with tears in my eyes for the beauty of it all. We hanker for power and control. The tough guy wants certainty, most of all about his power over others. And for a long time it seems he has it. Afterwards we find out he was a fraud, or everyone hated him so much that the moment he was gone they changed everything. He turned out to be a footprint in the sand an hour before high tide. (And the tide is so gentle, but relentless nevertheless.)

So, coming back to the city? When they said to me, "What are you doing here?" I thought of swimming in the creek the day after a flood, and I thought, "I have all that in my heart. And the job I am going to do is nothing like the job I would have done if I was twenty-five, and void of the experience I have."

Nevertheless, I had to stand tall in my aloneness. I had come to an ailing organisation, a container of fear and ugliness. Or, just the normal practice of modern-day management. I mentioned the following incident in *Sustenance*. An employee committed suicide. She took an overdose of sleeping pills. At ten o'clock in the morning in the office an announcement was made. A manager stood on a chair with the wondering staff gathered around him. He gave a brief précis of the facts. He was sorry, and expressed his condolences to the family. And that was it. Everyone returned to their desks.

The truth was... "The truth was...." Yes, the truth was, as I found out later, the person had been put under an immense amount of stress. I don't know the facts. Maybe she was out of touch with the job requirements, maybe she was incompetent, maybe she just couldn't handle stress very well. Or perhaps she had been put under inappropriate pressure by the new managerial regime, who thought that the way to change direction and increase profits was to demand more and push people hard, and let them know that everything they had been doing was wrong.

But there it was. A death in the morning, that shouldn't have been. It was just work. And in this company, if she had survived and come back to work, no one would have talked about it.

So everyone was silent, and there was such heartache in that silence. Because all the causes were still there. In the end, the tough guys become killers. (And afterwards, they kill themselves. What is there left to do?)

40

King Wen would say "Work on what has been spoiled. The bowl is full of worms and they are breeding." What does this mean? It is an analogy for false ideas about how things work. False ideas come from faulty perceptions, and the faulty perceptions lead to decay, breaking down, decomposition. I'd always felt that this perception that the world was tough and we have to beat it (and people) into submission, was wrong, but for the people who believe it, it is self-fulfilling.

Suppose the woman had not committed suicide. Suppose she had decided to turn her anger outwards instead of taking her own life. In this scenario she turns up at work with a gun and kills her most hated manager. Then everyone talks about the dangers of violence at work, and security measures multiply. The root problem never gets mentioned again. It is as if it gets locked up in a box and put away.

Yes, says King Wen. This is the bowl full of venomous creatures. All the things we lock up in a box and put away. The poisonous insects are feeding on faulty perceptions.

I'm not sorry I came back to the city. It was called for. People ask me, "Why did you come back?" and "Are you sorry you came back?" and "You don't have to stay. You could leave again."

I have been angry, and disgusted, and appalled. I have been amazed at the haplessness of many managers I have seen, who do not have the slightest of clues about how to relate to their employees with honesty and decency, and who do not even have much of a clue about doing business productively.

Yet their possession of power saves them from the consequences of what they do and what they create. When there is a problem, they have all the skills of pointing their finger at someone else to take the blame.

But is it so difficult to be a good manager? I go back to my books and delve among them, and I read, "Originally no one is deluded". I don't think about leaving the city again. Nor do I think about staying. It's just not what I am thinking about. I am thinking about this mystery of ordinary people

146

who become monsters, callous and mindless monsters, in this world of business culture, this prevailing delusion about annihilating your competitors, and in the process, brutalising your own employees.

There is no doubt that we construct the world that we live in. Yes, of course there is an "objective reality"; I am no solipsist. There are trees, and earth, and rain, and other people. I am a person with a body, residing and working in buildings. But what we do is create the meaning of it all, its significance. This is signified by the fact that we can look at one photograph and think it is ordinary, unexceptional, and then at another photograph and think it is moving and inspiring. Those qualities do not reside in the photographs, they reside in us.

We grow up and get a job in a company, and we learn the world that has been constructed there. We enter into it and become a member. We fulfil a role, a hole that was waiting for us to fill. The beliefs that prevail there, they came from the ideas that were floating around in earlier moments, and through incidents and interpretations and the contributions of individuals. And it sits up above everyone, like a giant sculpture that hangs in the air in the foyer, made of guts and hammers, reports and gadgets, rule books and corporate T-shirts, a questionable sexual episode involving a manager, a lie about a product, a sleazy sales tactic.

It all hangs up there like modern art that we don't pretend to understand but we assume is to be admired. It hangs up there like sadness, and you know that it is the roof that is holding all this up. But sometimes, the artist is just saying, "Here you are, this is for you" (meaning to say, "This *is* you") and she is not saying it is pretty. Perhaps what she would like best is if you tore it down.

147

I think, in my simplest moments, that if a manager were to say to me, "What should I do?" I would answer, "Say you're sorry. Say, 'I have been unkind'". But how can you do this when you think that cruelty is necessary? King Wen says change does not come through force. It comes through gentle penetration. The wind blows through the cracks in our fortress. Gently and consistently, it says the same thing, over and over, "Originally no one is deluded".

If this is true, what is this thing that we knew before we became deluded? I can tell you this about it: it means that you are taken care of. You can go out into this world and live boldly, freely, creatively. And ethically. Yes, knowing this thing would mean that you would live ethically. As Schweitzer said, with regard to the well-being of others.

What is the thing? Well, you already know it, but there is the dazzle of the corporate vision and there are the dark secrets that lurk behind its facade.

Bleak, my heart,
and wounded my days.
Sun in a falling sky,
the spell tightens.

We may have forgotten the truth, but at times we know the dirtiness of what we are doing. Like an executive of an asbestos company meeting a former employee in the last days of his life, hooked up to an oxygen tank. In such moments, all the justifications desert us, and we just hope for the moment to pass and we can pretend it did not happen, or that it did not mean what we think it might mean. We go home and lock the gate, and the door, and stare out over the harbour from our lounge room, wine glass in hand but strangely unmotivated, bereft of our usual assurance.

We are not all so prominent. Perhaps our sins are not quite so odious. And there is the obstinate belief that what we do is necessary, it is the only way. Besides, the ideals of the ethicists are ethereal dreams, mere longings for what cannot be in this world. This is a gritty world of steel and concrete and cash, not gossamer dancing on the village green.

41

There is something else. One of my daughters reminded me recently. She discovered the book and read it. Her verdict: you should read it, dad. Not that you'll agree with its perspective and its values, but you should know that this perspective is a major influence among people, especially in business. She was talking about *Atlas Shrugged*. The author: Ayn Rand.

I'd forgotten about this conversation too, until I was browsing at a market yesterday, and there it was on a stall. So I bought it and I've been dabbling. When I saw the book I realised it was part of the picture. I'd heard of the author, and I'd read about her philosophy, but I'd forgotten what a central part she played in the development of the managerial mindset.

You don't really get told about the roots of management when you study it at university. They tell you the functions of management and they tell you the major theories of management, but they are silent about its spiritual core. That you learn through osmosis after you get a job. You learn it from those who have imbibed it and learned its message, and discovered the bond of brotherhood it creates. And how could you not, when you are given to see yourself as a leader, a creator, and a necessity for the progress of the world? And that others are not as you are.

Atlas Shrugged. Remarkably, it was published in 1957. Not for Ayn Rand; she had been working on it since about 1946. But for us. It means that it was published in the same short period as other key concepts in management. Milton Friedman, Peter Drucker, Jacques Ellul. This is fascinating in terms of how certain concepts pour out into the world to contend, all around the same period in time. *Atlas Shrugged* is a novel, and Ayn Rand is adamant that she is first and foremost a novelist, but she is also quite clear that the novel is the representation of a philosophy, which she explicitly articulates.

Between *Atlas Shrugged*, *The Fountainhead* and her other works, Ayn Rand has sold more than twenty million books. There are numerous books about her and about her philosophy, which she called Objectivism, and there is an Ayn Rand Institute which promulgates her philosophy. It is a philosophy which demands to be preeminent, and it incorporates an ethic that underpins the philosophy with righteousness. Most of all, it carries the appeal of heroism. It is a set of beliefs that, imbibed well, can make you impervious to inconveniences like the inconsistency of reality with your beliefs.

"My philosophy, in essence, is the concept of man as a heroic being, with his own happiness as the moral purpose of his life, with productive achievement as his noblest activity, and reason as his only absolute." How enormously attractive. How wonderful to be given permission to make your own happiness your only ethical rule. How does this sit with the definition of ethics that Schweitzer gave us, that ethics is about concern for the well-being of others? Ayn

150

Rand gives us ethics with one hand, and takes it away with the other.

I realise that the advocates of this philosophy would probably respond that the philosophy is deeper than her statement here suggests, that it is more subtle and nuanced, and that I've misunderstood. I think the statement is clear enough and it has had its impact, on millions of managers and aspirants. She does say that she is talking about man as man, that is, the whole species of rational beings, but when she is asked to explain ethics she is blunt: "self-interest".

It makes a difference whether you understand this to mean I should act in the best interests of the species or just in the best interests of my own self. She says that man should "live for his own sake, neither sacrificing himself to others nor sacrificing others to himself", but on what grounds should I not sacrifice others to myself if that serves my happiness?

The answer given, I suppose, is that you would not sacrifice others to yourself because it would not be in the rational self-interest of man as man. But she explicitly rejects any form of altruism – morality for her does not consist in living for others or for society. Now, I think it might be possible for someone to interpret this philosophy in such a way that they do not set out to harm others, but I think you would not want to count upon them in a crisis. They would be taking a moment to rationally weigh up whether their happiness might be better served by not helping you.

But they would feel justified, and that's the important thing about a philosophy. This is an appealing philosophy because it is branded well. The name "Objectivism" broadcasts the claim that it is the only possible philosophy. Everyone else is subjective, that is, wrong. But I think, what would Theodore

151

Roszak have to say about this? "Objective" turns out not to be so objective when you look it in the eye.

Think of a chair. There couldn't be much argument about a chair, could there? Until I take this chair and visit an aboriginal tribe that doesn't have chairs. They look at it, and they see, at most, a strange configuration of wood that has no purpose and is of only passing curiosity. You protest. You say, the chair is still the chair. If they came into our world they would understand what a chair is. And I say, that's exactly right. The only way they can give sense to a chair is by coming into our world.

This is what the objectivist does. He demands that you come into his (her) world and accept all of his meanings. But the reciprocal courtesy is not given. Nothing about the aboriginal view of the world is granted. It is all branded as.... What? Naïve, primitive, superstitious, uninformed? But when I say to the Objectivist, "Your philosophy is just a story; in fact, it is just another story", who turns out to be naïve, primitive, superstitious and uninformed then? Particularly if we consider that the mad thrust of "progress" seems to be plunging us rapidly towards global climatic upheaval.

These meanings, the meanings that the objectivist glosses over and assumes, they are poor things, they are sentimental things wrapped in an unexamined culture. They are self-serving, although I guess they would see this as appropriate. But they do not want you to see these meanings as self-serving; they want you to see them as "objective". And I wonder what camaraderie is like among the self-serving? Do they accept the sword thrust from a comrade gladly, knowing that it serves the greater good of their heroic destiny? That there is a small elite that will prevail, even if some of them have to die at each other's hands to enable its fulfilment?

Yes, there is a pathway away from superstition that we ought to take. It would be foolish not to do so. The earth, we have learned, is not flat. It is a round thing. And it is not held up by elephants and a turtle. Nor is it held up by Atlas. That too is a mythology. When Ayn Rand tells us, in a thousand pages of a novel, that the elite capitalists are the chosen ones with clear minds who make the world work, this is a mythology. What is unfortunate about it is that it has spawned a generation of self-serving leaders who believe that their destiny is to build their palaces on the bones of those they use and abuse.

Having said all this, I need to say that I don't think most managers subscribe to this notion. Most people have not formulated their philosophy with such clarity, and their beliefs are a brawling mix of contradictions that surface at different times in different situations. But I think the ideas of Objectivism lurk in the background, they are like a minute amount of poison that is in the water supply. We are all drinking in small doses of it all the time, and it has its influence because our bodies are prone to it.

Most times, managers manage to be at least half-way decent. The urge to treat other people decently is innately very strong, and apart from that, most managers know that you are more likely to achieve good results if you work harmoniously with people rather than bullying them. When harshness and bullying are rampant it is generally a sign of widespread stress in the organisation. No, I would say it more strongly: it is a sign that at the cultural level, the organisation is seized by a crisis – of survival, of identity or of faith.

153

42

So, the message is simple. The bird sits in the tree, calling. Our life is the story that we make. It can be true or untrue, that is one criterion. But it can be exalted or moribund. That is the other criterion. The life that you make is the life that you live with, and the life that you die with.

This is so at a personal level. But then we work for organisations, and they are subject to mythologies. You understand that a mythology is a story? It is a way that we represent the nature of reality. And it can be true or untrue, according to (a) how well it accommodates the "objective" facts we know, and (b) how well it accords with ethics, that is, how much it has regard for the well-being of all-that-is.

Qualifications and clarifications. We need to have some humility about so-called objective facts. They have a habit of changing. At one time, the earth was held to be flat. Now it is round. At one time, people who behaved in certain ways were considered to be (literally) possessed by a devil. Now we have a variety of psychological understandings about what may be happening to the person. It is best to retain a little humility in the face of "facts".

I place ethics here to bring the yin-yang notion before you again. When we just talk about the heroic aspect of leadership, the vision it is striving to achieve, we forget the other half of the bargain – ethics, or, the manner in which we will do our striving. It is in the nature of the reality we are given that the yang of goal-striving is married to the constraint of morality. The most common mistake of our mythologies of leadership is that they put all the emphasis on action and not enough on reflection. We favour the decisive manager who makes up his (her) mind instantly and plunges the organisation into action. We neglect the aspect of looking carefully and considering what is happening before we make up our mind.

This is true in a strategic sense. We have to get that it also applies in the ethical sense. In the strategic sense it means that we stop to think about the whole situation before we dive in. I'm told that fire fighters are trained to stop when they get to the fire scene, not to dive in and start doing things. This may happen very quickly, in the fire fighter's mind, but it is a habit that reminds the fire fighter to ask, "Is this really what I am seeing? Is there something deceptive here? Am I taking everything into account?" and I would include ethics at this point, the questions about whether someone is being treated unfairly, whether there are people who need to be protected or helped or safeguarded. Ethics is not an after-thought; it is part of the parcel of leadership.

I think part of the reason that ethics has been marginalised is because of the mythologies we have about reason. Again, Ayn Rand has played a big hand in this. Her vision is that the great leader is guided solely by reason. She says man's reason is fully competent to know the facts of reality, and it is the only means of acquiring knowledge. Reason, she says, is also the only proper judge of values.

I think enough has been written just in the last twenty years to show that this is a very inadequate depiction of reality and a very inadequate guide to action. Nevertheless, in ordinary parlance it retains its power. It persists like a bad habit.

Here's an example of how our actions are not adequately explained by reason. A neonatal nurse observes a baby in a humidicrib and says to the doctor, "This baby is showing signs of an impending crisis. We should do something now." The doctor can't see it. Nothing is untoward on any of the monitoring charts.

155

Yet the nurse is right – before long, the baby starts to show signs of stress. Was the nurse psychic? Gary Klein wrote about studies conducted with all sorts of hands-on professionals like neonatal nurses. He said these nurses simply got very good at observing babies, and could pick up subtle patterns long before others could, including doctors, who didn't have the chance to watch babies so closely.

The nurses weren't doing the "rational" thing – gathering facts, weighing up the positives and negatives, and deciding on a rational choice. They were observing closely and learning to recognise patterns of behaviour. Isn't this fantastic? This is a different way of understanding. It doesn't make us irrational, but it enlarges our understanding of what "reason" means. Significantly. Hugely. It means our reason functions best as the servant of qualities like empathy and learned intuition. We seek to understand something and we learn the patterns of its behaviour. Our heart must be engaged as well as our cognitive skills. It is all connected, seamless.

And likewise, ethics is part of the seamless whole.

The business world I came back to is a world of damage. It is a world where only one in six employees can be described as "fully engaged". The engagement chart is a bell curve that sounds like a death knoll. Organisations carry the weight of all that apathy, sullenness, resistance and, at the extreme, revulsion. Most managers and leaders are only capable of maintaining a system; they are not capable of reshaping it.

To reshape an organisational environment takes a vision that is large enough to contain and transform the downward pull of the current energy level in the organisation. It is like healing a sickness. And having a vision is not enough. A vision is what the alternative settlers had when they left the city and took to the land. Then they discovered (some of them) that they had brought all their old mental models and patterns of behaviour with them. It was enough to tear the vision apart, or corrode it slowly.

I still have dreams about how ugly life can be as an employee in an organisation. I am sitting in a communal space in a prison camp. A woman prisoner walks back into the room. She has been at an interrogation interview. The questions asked of her have been accusatory. Her version of events has been disputed. Her report on the incident has been mysteriously lost. Vicious witnesses have concocted stories against her. The interrogator is a smiler. He drives a fancy car.

When the woman walks back into the room she is carrying a handful of filthy paper. She doesn't want to talk. She goes out of the room to a toilet. The interrogators are going to make her eat all of this filthy paper, to swallow it. It will make her vomit. Then their job will be done.

Not a pretty dream. But salient. Too close to reality for many employees, who serve managers who think they are doing what needs to be done, but it seems that this necessitates lying, and bullying those who do the actual work of the organisation. It is a belief that is so very convenient for them. At the end of office hours, the managers drive away in their very shiny cars that the company has bought for them.

43

If I wanted to change an organisation, I would start with ethics. I would start with standards of conduct. I would announce that lying and bullying are pathological behaviour, and they are unacceptable methods for "getting the job done". This is where I would start, regardless of the supposed crises that were going on. Supposing there was a crisis, why would employees want to help the leader?

Oh, yes, of course, out of fear for their own jobs. Well, just remember the bell curve. In most organisations, only about 15% of the energy is working for you, and most of that is coming from managers who have power they can exercise over others, or professionals who have some measure of autonomy. The other 85% is either passive or is actively against you. Good luck.

One of the major reasons for reason is to justify the pathological behaviour of the leader. The appeal to reason is an ideological assertion that masks greed, stupidity, laziness and a host of other ills. True reason is signified by the attentiveness to detail of a nurse watching the breathing of a new baby, it is the scanning of the entire scene that a fire fighter does when he arrives at the location of a fire. Reason is a tool in service of awareness and human values, it is not an end in itself, or a tool devoid of context. The nurse only learns about babies because she (he) cares about the individual human life. The fire fighter only learns about fires because he (she) cares about preventing destruction and protecting life from danger.

Leaders generally don't want to think that they might be pathological. But it is worth thinking about. Don't blame yourself entirely, the situation probably existed that way before you arrived. You just picked it up and have kept it going. And you thought it was all necessary if the organisation was going to survive. Even the riches that go those at the top, you thought that was all necessary too. You thought that this was part of the necessary structure of things. It is a whole construct that you don't want to dismantle, because then everything might fall apart. You

158

probably also have an obligation to the structure of things to accept an astronomical salary.

I am simply saying, causing harm to people, knowingly, continually, as an entrenched pattern of behaviour, is pathological, no matter what the context. The fact that it is an accepted more of the business world does not stop it from being pathological. The argument that it is necessary does not stop the behaviour from being pathological. It is a sickness. The fact that it is widely practised and that it is accepted as a norm just means that this sickness is widespread.

The mental model of Big Circle–Little Circle exposes the sickness. We have allowed ourselves to believe that Business is the Big Circle, and human life is just a Little Circle within it. We have allowed ourselves to believe.... So we are responsible for how things are, all of it. I am just saying the reality is, all those human values – honesty, compassion, integrity, sincerity, humility, politeness, decency, fairness, patience, respect, justice, graciousness, kindness, appreciation, equanimity, loyalty – they all apply, everywhere inside the Big Circle, which is all of human life, that comes before any particular activity in which we might engage, for example, sport, recreation, musical performance, community celebrations – or business.

Saying that it is necessary to treat people badly is not a truth, it is a fatuous ideology.

Are things getting better or worse? I'm not a believer in either "things are getting worse" or "things are getting better". I think that both of those mindsets are artefacts in the minds of journalists and commentators, to create a premise for articles. I think things are always getting better, and always getting worse, at the same time. It's a question of what you

159

choose to focus on, and on what you can do to change your particular context.

However, I think that the pace of change, and the fact that in a globalised environment, our context is always being absorbed into a larger context, gives people the excuse not to think about the quality of their leadership. They think, there's too much going on, let's just get the next six months of business changes out of the way, then we can think about the way we're doing things. Ha! You are dooming yourself to be like this forever. And it means you continue to perpetuate all the unsavouriness of the current behaviour of leaders.

Is it all too hard? No, it's not. Yes, there is a sense in which, in the end, we will have to remake our organisations completely, we will have to, as Kahlil Gibran says in *The Prophet*, unpick the cloth strand by strand. But small changes can begin to remake the world. I have said, "Start with ethics". But how? I say, first, if there is something you are doing that you know is wrong, stop doing it, now. Don't be afraid. You may be surprised at the positive effect.

I remember, when I was teaching high school, that I struggled with the great bogey of young teachers, classroom control. And one day I was shouting at the kids and I suddenly thought, this is crazy. That's not enough, generally, to stop a person doing what they are in the midst of doing. But I did. I just stopped. Not in defeat, but in recognition that shouting was not the way to go on. It was unhealthy, and if I continued to shout, the shouting would just go on, and the riotness and everything that went with it.

Remarkably, the classroom went quiet. The students looked at me questioningly and then I talked to them, calmly. It didn't mean that the problem was suddenly solved completely, but we did work together a lot better after that. We learned to accommodate each other's needs and work productively together. That moment was the beginning of the change. Nor did I see this as a "triumph of reason". I don't find that a very helpful way to look at it. Rather, it was what I just said, a recognition of each other's needs and a commitment to work together. That's more about love than reason.

So, step one: stop doing what you know is wrong. (This means we accept that all those laws of ethics apply everywhere; you are always inside the Big Circle.)

Step two is also simple. Consider a few of the human values – basic, important ones, and start practising them. For example, think of kindness. How are you currently being unkind? How could you be kinder to those around you? This is not to promote weakness or sentimentality. Yes, many work environments are inherently robust. That's fine. But kindness belongs everywhere; you are always inside the Big Circle. As the Dalai Lama said, the only religion humanity needs is the religion of kindness. Being successful and being kind as well, what could be better?

44

But could you be successful if you were maintaining ethics in your conduct? This is really the question, isn't it? This is life's biggest question, as long as you live in the world. It may also apply to the hermit in a cave, but it certainly stands in the way of anyone who works in the world of business, like a monster blocking your path.

We know this because of the number of books and articles that try to persuade us that it really is in our best interests to be ethical: "Is ethics good for business?" There are studies. The empiricists have looked at companies that have instituted a range of formal ethics measures, and mapped this against their performance on the stock market. The formal measures have included having a code of ethics, implementing ethics training programs, having an ethics officer, or an ethics "Hotline" where employees can anonymously report corrupt practices. Et cetera. You get the idea.

Studies like this tend to show that the companies who have undertaken formal measures to promote ethical conduct by employees do perform better than average on the stock market. Well, then, you think, perhaps I should tend towards introducing some ethics measures into my company. There is a likelihood that it will be good for business. And you can see the problem immediately.

If the evidence had been otherwise, it would be perfectly sensible, indeed, good business practice, not to be ethical (speaking crudely; we just mean that it would not make business sense to introduce any formal ethics measures). At some point in this train of thinking it will occur to you that ethics cannot be treated in this way. There is no conditionality about ethics. If it applies at all, it applies regardless of outcomes, otherwise it is not ethics. It is, well, business.

I don't accuse the authors of these studies of being simple-minded, or of ignoring this central fact. But it is about the message that ends up being portrayed: good ethics = good business. It's just that the moment you admit this logic, you have to accept the converse: if the evidence for the proposition turns out to be not compelling enough, then it makes it a bad business decision to be ethical. It's the very admission of business logic to the question that is misguided. Ethics is a different kind of proposition.

The deeper message is that there is something very teasing about the results of these studies. In fact, it seems as if there could be some kind of virtuous relationship between ethical behaviour and business success. Any business person who has any conscience still breathing inside him/her would be interested in exploring this further, would want to understand – what is the connection between them?

One of the stories that stands tall in the literature of business ethics is the story of Johnson & Johnson's product Tylenol, a pain reliever. In the early 1980s an incident occurred where a number of people in the same area in the US died of poisoning over a short period of time. Upon investigation, it was discovered that the common factor was Tylenol. The product had been tampered with, and cyanide added. It was not known who did it or how.

Presented with the evidence, Johnson & Johnson was faced with a crisis. This product was one of its main revenue-earners. It had to decide what to do, and quickly. The total cost to the company of taking the product off the market was estimated at around $100 million. The company's decision has achieved legendary status, as it famously decided, voluntarily, to immediately withdraw all Tylenol from sale until the culprits were found or the problem of tampering was solved. The company worked to develop tamper-proof packaging and then re-introduced the product. Its reputation as a trusted provider of pharmaceuticals recovered, and it easily recaptured its market share, and its profit levels. (Strangely, the culprits were never found.)

What was central to this story was the company's rationale for withdrawing Tylenol from sale. It said it had a responsibility to safeguard the health of its customers, and this responsibility was paramount. Until it could ensure the safety of the product, it would not allow it to be sold. The cost of the recall was not a factor in the decision, although of course the executives were very conscious of the cost and of the threat to the future of the company.

In retrospect, it's easy to say that the recall was the smart business decision. You could say that putting customers at risk of poisoning was not in Johnson & Johnson's best interests in the long term, so they were in fact acting prudently. But to emphasise the long-term outcome is to miss the point of the story.

When the company pulled the product off the market, it sustained an immediate, huge loss, and there was no promise of recovery. Johnson & Johnson could have collapsed. If you were one of the executives making this decision, you could not have argued that you knew things would be alright in the long run. All they had at that moment was their moral principles. Later, one of the executives revealed that they knew what they had to do (morally), but they were scared about the company's financial future.

Could you have made this decision if you had a contingent attitude towards ethics? If you'd put a price on it? You would have buckled, and this is the difference your decision would have made. If you had decided to be expedient about this situation, and bluff your way through with the public and with regulators, all of the company's energy in those weeks would have gone into damage control.

You would have had to spend big dollars on advertising that reassured the public, you would have had to concoct a suitably soothing message for employees. Your salespeople would have had to spend many hours delivering carefully scripted messages to doctors and pharmacies everywhere. You would have to hope that nobody slipped up, and you would have to hope above all that nothing else happened, like another death.

What happened at Johnson & Johnson, in contrast? The energy went into innovation. In just a few weeks, the engineers had developed tamper-proof packaging. Not perfect, nothing can be in this area, but robust. This is the difference when people make a conscious decision to act ethically. Good, constructive energy is liberated, rather than the furtive, watch-your-back energy that is generated when self-interest dominates (at someone else's expense) and deceit is necessary.

Sure, the fear was there, because the future was uncertain – the company's efforts might still not be good enough, and circumstances might still militate against it. But one thing the company's executives could be sure of: they would not be in danger of waking up one morning with a spotlight in their face and a reporter exposing their lies and actions that led to the death of another customer. Honest people sleep better, even when things are not going well.

45

I am aware that what I've just been saying might seem preachy. Should I apologise, or recant? No. If you've got to this point you've survived. It's just that I'm taking stock, and last time I checked, I was slowing down, staying at home. Doing last checks on my PhD proposal. Perhaps you are wondering what has been happening.

It's the same, only calmer. I have tidied up some parts of the house and it feels orderly. I have resurrected some garden space and planted new flowers, and it feels nourishing (aesthetics can do that). I have had a fence built along one boundary of my property, to keep the busy road out, and now my space is enclosed and it feels like a sanctuary. Do you think that Ayn Rand devotees have such pleasures? I think they might; it's just hard to reconcile it with being a ruler of the world.

The birds have been quiet. It is raining again. It has rained day and night, but now, in the evening, the rain is having a rest, as the darkness gathers. Yesterday I saw a kookaburra, sitting on a wire. The wire was swaying back and forth, and the kookaburra was swaying back and forth with it. This is how the world works. It is only humans who make up stories about the world that deny the wisdom of kookaburras.

The shape of sky

I have pondered the shape of sky
poured down cracks between buildings,
leaning on trees,
a blank canvas for the sun,
a host for clouds.
I have seen the sky angular,
and as the softest margin over far hills.
I ponder the shape of sky,
patient with the limits I set for it.

I realise that it must be disorienting for some readers, even annoying, when I pause to ponder the shape of sky. I argue that the shape of sky (as I have defined it) tells us many things. Eventually it will tell you that you have to laugh at humans and what they do. In the vastness of that deep blue we call sky, the meagre fragment of blue between one building and another is nothing. And here you are watching it (now that I have made you aware of it, the blue between buildings).

We devote so much of our time to being a master of the universe, or at least a small part of it, when what we need to do is to be wistful. Ah, what a responsibility!

46

In fact, all this time I have been mulling over a story I wrote, and whether it belongs here. I've already come out, as it were, and discussed some of my stories, that come from my Secluded Period. I'm committed to including a couple of them at the end, as a homage to Herman Hesse. So, let me talk about this particular story.

I used to write in winter, sitting on the lounge room floor, alone in my house in the valley, with the fire alight, burning logs that came from trees on the hills around me. (Do you see why I find the business world so arid? Do you see why I get exasperated by the concept of holidays? I live in a place where people ache to go on holidays, whereas I was already living in a place where I wanted to be.)

I never had a plan. I never composed it like some writers do, in their head, on the bus. I would sit down on the floor with a writing pad and a pen in the evening. The page would be blank. It would be dark outside, and silent. Oftentimes, I would write rubbish, wandering drivel, and then I would screw it up and throw it into the fire (sometimes you never get near the gate, but at least you are close to the grate).

Mostly I would invent a person first, and give him/her a name. The name gave them a feeling, it might even suggest a cultural space. And then I would put them into action, inventing an environment around them, and a situation, word by word, sentence by sentence. I would play with sounds. There were sounds I did not like, and sounds I was attracted to.

One night I summoned "Yunwin". She took shape as a young girl. I had no personal reference points for her. She was not like a sister, mother, daughter, or daughter of a friend. She was a stranger to me. But I felt with her.

She was the daughter of two sad and harsh parents, living in a forest. I did not know why they were like that. And she went into the forest one day, and became lost. She met a strange man, who was like a guru, except that all he did was chant for several hours each day. Nothing else: no teachings, no followers. Just the chanting. And she followed him. Oddly, she was not like a disciple, she was more like a keeper. She looked after him – it can be dangerous when you are just sitting in a forest chanting. Wild beasts might attack you while you are defenceless.

This went on for months. Each day, the chanting, and then Yunwin would find food for them both, and they would go on their way. After what seemed like a long time, she found herself near her forest home, and she went to visit her parents. She found that her mother had died, and her father was there alone. He was still gruff with her; he always had been, at the best of times. But here was the interesting thing – although he was gruff, there was no energy in his gruffness. It was as if he was only gruff out of habit. He did not know how to do otherwise. But, finally, now, he meant her no harm. The energy had gone out of the cruelty.

She prepared a fine pot of soup for him before she left.

So yes, I will include the story at the end of this book. You already know my appreciation for soup.

But you ask, what happens next? And why this story? What is it about?

I know this much. Here we are, all of us, and we have been following mad demons. We have been deluded, hypnotised. Our behaviour has been atrocious. We have been so thoughtless, so cruel. We have tried to persuade ourselves that it was with the best of intentions, but we know better. Or we have fabricated the most magnificent of justifications. But we know how hollow they are. And we have built all of our behaviours into habits, and to our horror, even when we start to think differently, the habits continue. We think fine thoughts, and then we turn around and say something cruel to our partner, our colleague, our friend.

This, I think, is partly what Yunwin is about. The story asks us to recognise that often we are trying to change, but we are still running on habit. And anyway, why should other people think we are changing, when we have been this way for years? Sensitive, isn't it? The beauty of Yunwin is that she felt the change in her father in her heart. That was why she made the soup for him. She couldn't say anything, that was beyond what was possible, but she could make soup. And for days, her father would eat that soup and be nourished by it.

I feel there is much more to Yunwin, but I can't, no, I haven't been able yet, to take the story further. There is much more to be told.

But, the next question, what has this got to do with business and leadership?

Okay, I'll try to answer. I can say this: given that we are all here now, we all stand here with a history, and it's safe to assume that the history is messy, and everyone around us knows it. So everyone around us has perceptions about who we are, what we are like, and that sets a limit on what we can do.

So in the middle of this, we decide that we will be different – better. And we announce the new principles: I will be honest, caring, consultative, collaborative, encouraging. Soon afterwards, our entrenched habits ensure that we have a relapse. So far, no one has any evidence that we have changed at all, and in fact it is worse, because now they think we are playing a new scam, with all this talk about caring and honesty.

And at this point I'd like to talk about the "guru" in the story, whose name is Mu (in the I Ching, Mu stands for "world tree", which I didn't know at the time I wrote the story, but I accept the meaning gratefully). All Mu does is chant. I think his chanting stands for a persistent reaffirmation of the positive (for the religious, this would be God; for those who are more diffusively spiritual, this could be the angels of kindness, or the values of loving kindness). It is the chant of those who are deep in their sin, or their habits, and who know that this is all they can do at the moment. But the blessing is that this is enough for them, if they will but come back and chant each day.

Mu, the guru, is in fact us in our imperfection. He is not an exalted being, except insofar as he shows us a way. A way forward. And no, it wasn't written for the business world or for managers. But yes, it applies. No one in the business world is going to talk to you about operating ethically. And what does Mu tell us? He tells us that we have done wrong, we do wrong every day. And it is not unavoidable wrong. We have done wrong in the sense that we should not have done wrong, and we are responsible for the results – the hurt, the disappointment, the dismay we cause in others.

The seduction of reason is the rationalisations it continually offers us. Mu couldn't care less about your reasons. He asks whether you have hurt anybody recently. He waits for your answer. He is willing to wait a long time, and all of that time his eyes watch you. And the worst of it is, he is watching you with love, so much love. Is it any wonder that Yunwin went home and found that the fire had gone out of her father's anger? Her father had not yet found a new dawn, but there was nothing to sustain the darkness except the habits of years.

Into this space we must sing.

47

It seems that we must live in cities (the bulk of us) and do business with one another. We congregate, aggregate, accumulate and gesticulate. It is unfortunate that most of our conversations are built upon faulty foundations, false mental models of the nature of the world and the nature of persons and society. The words we use with each other have been perfected to enable superficial transactions but leave the assumptions unquestioned. Fish never talk about water, they just swim in it.

King Wen says that this is the quest: to take to the tower and watch – watch yourself and what you do, watch how others deal with one another, listen to the birds. Observe and ponder. You will learn many things. Sometimes, there is no Right Thing to do, and you must sit with your not-knowing. Sometimes, you will see, there is only one thing to be done, which is the Right Thing, and you must do it. At such times, keep your ego in check with your reins.

What should you ask, when you are sitting in the tower? I think this is a good question to be asking: is what you are doing nourishing you (you, the soul in there, not the ego)? If it does not nourish you, it cannot stir up new growth. And suppose you get an unpleasant answer to your question. What then? King Wen says, this could be a crisis. You need to gather all of your strength. Hold onto your ideals. Don't be afraid to break the rules. Become an individual. This could be a major transition. One thing is finished, you are stepping across a threshold, and you are a new seed. Stand by what you know to be true. Accept the movement.

Here is a new project: harmonise Heaven and Earth. Go to your work, go to your organisation, go to your business, and do that. Unmake the damage, and make Heaven and Earth sing in what you do.

Practise, repeat, rehearse. Shine.

48

To end properly, we should go back to the beginning, and see how far we've come. Perhaps it will not matter, perhaps we have changed so much that what we thought at the beginning is now irrelevant. But even then, it is good to know this. Accordingly, I have gone back, and searched among my early writings to see if there is anything that still rings true.

This is what I found.

Celebration
"Come and join the living." (Cat Stevens)

If father sitting slippered by the fire
should ask me,
I would probably not be able to tell him
all the things I have seen,
all the shapes I have taken and discarded:

I padded through the grass
and watched show after show
from the outside of the circle.
I learned your cunning
but I do not use it,

my sides are pinched,
I have fasted voluntarily.

Tempting it is to make my revelation:
I have been to the top of the mountain.
But you tell me there is no mountain.
What is it you want?
Why do you eye me as if
I would steal the acrid wind from your lungs?

As it is I am
air, the spirit of the summits and the valleys;
I will slip through your fingers.
I mad? Listen, dead man, it is
your own sly brothers
who have followed me with cameras
and sold my pictures to the devil,
but your brothers do not know
the other half of the transaction.
It is your small soul
that you do not know about
that is reflected in my eyes,
or else, why do you watch me so?

I dance because you are a cripple.
I laugh because I can slip
through the bars of any cage
and watch you from the outside.
We have been through your madness
and our own despair.
Of course, no one has said you couldn't come
to join the celebration,
but we shan't wait for you to start,
for you might never come.

So it is true – what I have to say is not much
different to what I said a long time ago, as a young
man, even before I went bush. (Pedantic note: The

"father" in the poem is not my father, it is a representation of society. I probably didn't need to say this, but it would also be wrong if you thought I had a conflict with my father, who rests in peace.) I say it again, now, having been away and come back. I say it in this world of cities and business, because it seems the same arid and destructive illusions continue to hold sway.

Heaven above the mountain. Retreating to reflect on the matter at hand is the adequate first step in any action.

THE STORIES

Prevailing Myths

Rambril's Story

Yunwin

Prevailing Myths

Krauwing stood on the edge of the world. All he could see was a multitude of places where he could fall. He waited for the fall, which didn't come.

Still he refused to believe. "The fall has not come *yet*," he said. Still it did not come. It was taking a long time.

A memory of a lady said to him, "Alright, while you are waiting, consider: suppose you fall. Let's say, down this way..."

And Krauwing knew what she was thinking: "You will recover".

"The fall I am thinking of," said Krauwing, "is worse than all of these. I'd like to know, is there something I can do to prevent it?"

Krauwing was just wondering if the lady would say, "Yes, there is a way," but before the lady had time to answer, a little man appeared.

"Hello," he said. "Don't stand there like that. You'll fall."

"I think I will leave your question unanswered," said the memory of a lady.

"Was there a question?" asked the little man.

"No," said Krauwing. "I have just altered my stance, and things look different."

*   *   *   *   *

Some myths are more prevailing than others. Of course. People are easily fooled. (Notoriously so.) And myths tend heavily to be constructed in terms of physical reality. Objects fall. Paint peels. Sleeping giants waken when you make a noise.

Krauwing painted his house twice a year to prove that paint does not peel. He banged kettles at night to prove that giants are sound sleepers.

He continues to exist. For Krauwing, continuing to exist is his forte. He exists in the same manner as levitated saints, unexploded bombs, uncut flowers.

If someone said, "Krauwing, you are about to fall," Krauwing would answer him. Or her.

There were no set answers. Generally Krauwing had dispensed with such, for he aimed to avoid the ordinary. There were others who could do the ordinary quite well.

"There are no rules," he said. "There are only people."

But there were standards that he followed. Two, in fact: to maintain decorum, and to avoid being tedious. Even though tedium is mostly in the mind of the beholder, and decorum, on the other hand, generally is not. There is no decorum; instead, there are people.

"Krauwing, you are falling."

"No," said Krauwing, "I am not falling."

"Why are the objects flying past you?"

"Are they? Look again."

Krauwing is not crazy. It is his belief that maintains his existence. Without that belief he would implode, he would become a black hole in front of an audience, he would be a non-contagious but fatal disease.

Krauwing fails to fall. Tedium is in the mind of the beholder, together with doubt and mistrust. Krauwing finds a gap in the wall, narrow enough to miss, so he is grateful to have found it. He squeezes through, and he has to be unnoticed. So he learns to be furtive, he learns tricks of invisibility.

When someone comes by, he is just sitting. "Krauwing", they say, "aren't you the one who fell?"

Krauwing tries to be honest. "I don't remember very well."

"Yes, it was you," says the passer-by. And the passer-by proceeds to ask questions, about falling, what it was like, and so on. None of which Krauwing answers. To which the response is growing anger.

"It is best not to ever get angry," was all that Krauwing said. The passer-by was disgusted, and left that way. Krauwing resumed his study of the gap in the wall. Vision is like that. Not something you can take for granted.

"Did you see that?" Krauwing says to a stranger.

"What was it?"

"No? Oh well, next time." He draws abuse for this speech. The stranger punches words at him – rude, supercilious, arrogant, smug. It is quite a list. Krauwing sits down to work through it. He inspects himself carefully for symptoms of the offending diseases.

He learns, when you see a gap in the wall, make sure someone else sees it before you mention it. Don't even mention it then. Let them say, "Hey, did you see this?" and be pleased about it. Then they will like you. There is no decorum, there are only people. Tedium is in the mind of the beholder.

A lady came by. "Looking for something?" she asked.

"I fell over," said Krauwing, "and I was trying to find the rock that I tripped on."

The lady gave a puzzled laugh. Krauwing relaxed.

"According to all the prevailing myths," said the lady, "that is a waste of time."

"Some myths are more prevailing than others," he replied. He bent down again as if looking for the rock.

"I don't think the rock is here," suggested the lady.

"No," said Krauwing, and he heaped abuse on the rock for its lack of responsibility. To the lady he apologised and said, "You probably think I'm rude, supercilious, arrogant and smug."

But the lady had a better idea of what she thought than did Krauwing. And having a sense of decorum, she did not tell him what she thought. Krauwing approved. They talked longer.

Then the lady asked him again, "What were you doing when I came?"

Krauwing said, "I have lost sight of the gap in the wall." And perhaps he had. Or perhaps, too, he wanted the lady to tell him she'd found it and be pleased about it.

The surprising thing, though, was that the lady did not seem to have any interest at all in the gap in the wall. He decided to think about this.

The lady was looking at a flower. "See," she said. "This is such a lovely flower." And it was, and it carried a scent of penetrating beauty. Krauwing thought, "Am I learning new things here?"

But after a minute he decided, "No, I will not be side-tracked into conversation. It is a good time for reaching."

And it was a good time. The lady saw it too, and dropped the flower. The flower was not important. Perhaps there were no memories inside her to echo what happened then with Krauwing, but the time was good enough to send its own ripples outwards, to the future and to the past. Didn't that amount to the same thing?

"One doesn't always just look through gaps in the wall," whispered the lady in his ear.

"No," said Krauwing. "No...."

*　　*　　*　　*　　*

In the morning the wall was solid. The gap was nowhere to be seen. Krauwing was grateful for the wall; there were some plants that needed a wall to grow up against. He set about digging and putting in shrubs and flowers.

Of course there were still passers-by. But they only saw some things. Krauwing no longer took vision for granted.

"Aren't you the one who fell?" said one.

Krauwing laughed gently. "You must be mistaken."

"No." The passer-by was sure of it. "You are the one. How did you recover?" And so on and so on.

Krauwing snapped back. He remonstrated, abused and belittled the passer-by at great length until it was clear that the passer-by was stung. The passer-by excused himself and left smartly.

Krauwing smiled at a flower. It would take the passer-by a long time of thinking to understand what the attack had been about. He would probably find all the reasons in Krauwing rather than himself. Well, that would be ordinary enough. Tedium is in the mind of the beholder.

He tapped the wall. It was solid. Soon it would be garlanded with blossoms. "Let there be new prevailing myths," he decreed, smiling.

*   *   *   *   *

Rambril's Story

Rambril first met Shar in the garden. He was with Dahl and Betty at the time. Dahl had received his name after his time in Asia. It had not been a happy time. Betty made up for it, consciously. Dahl was rebuilding, still occasionally pursued by fears impregnated in him in Asia.

Rambril had come to meet Shar. She was in the garden. He had been coming for weeks, and she was tending the garden – the vegetables and flowers – naked except for her panties. Her body was lithe, her eyes were serious and her cheekbones high, but not haughty.

She greeted him as a creature of the garden, soil on her hands, sawdust and mulch about her toes. Betty talked. It was just another afternoon. Shar was interested, and asked Rambril questions. The garden was curled, rolled and wrapped in green. Shar talked and watered, listened and weeded.

Dahl spoke from his own special place, wounded but tenacious, hurt, intermittently hopeful. The sun zoomed in from the hilltop and told them all it was time to move. So they took leave of Shar and walked back up the hill.

Betty spoke to Rambril. "I light the fire. I cook tea. I wash. The days pass, they become real. Dahl comes down to earth. When he doesn't I am helpless."

"Ah," said Rambril, "but you are not Asia, and you are real. Remember that you are real."

Dahl approached. "Serious?" he asked. "Come on, we will sing songs." And sing songs they did, a trio of voices in the shadows among the trees, as cheerful as a camp-fire.

Shar was somewhere else, crying songs to the sun, which had gone but for a while.

"Dahl," said Betty, "there is a tiger outside the door. What should we do?"

Dahl was thrown into pain. His breath was arrested, his heart-beat could almost be felt in the room. Gradually his eyes came back, to focus very strongly on Betty and Rambril both. "Sometimes when one is a warrior, one finds oneself to be the stronger. Sometimes one finds oneself to be the weaker. But when one has no desire to kill, the one situation is as intolerable as the other. And when one is torn to the heart, it is necessary to ask, 'Am I ready to die?'"

And Rambril could see that Betty was asking herself, "Am I ready to deny the existence of a tiger?"

Rambril took the door and ventured forth; if only because of the weariness in Betty's eyes. That night the tiger eluded him. He found himself at the door of Shar's house.

Shar was clothed against the cold. She showed no fear. "It is only I," said Rambril.

"Come in," she said.

Rambril entered. There were no tigers behind him, but it seemed to him that Shar looked to make sure. If one is not going to be afraid, then one has to be careful.

"It is alright," said Rambril. "There are no tigers."

"I like to make sure," replied Shar.

Rambril sat by the fire. He thought about the qualities of warriors. "But first of all," he thought, "it is necessary to be human. At one point the strength of the superior warrior turns into the hardness of the defective human." He looked again at Shar.

She questioned him.

"No judgement," he said, having looked again. But silently he challenged her.

Shar served wine and they drank. They talked in abstractions without getting lost. "Life is only possible if there is tension," said Rambril.

"But one must learn to relax," answered Shar. They sipped wine, and stared into flames. Certain rhythms maintained their cadence. Peacefulness was there in the movement. That night the movement was small, and they did not upset it. Rambril let go of assertiveness, as Shar already seemed to have done.

Rambril saw Shar from the top of the hill. She seemed grey and worn in a grey morning's light. Dahl was beside him. After all, perhaps the tiger waited in the shadows.

"Why the greyness?" Rambril asked Dahl.

Dahl thought that Rambril was referring to him. (That didn't matter.) "Possibly just a matter of bad planning. One should set goals, strive to reach them, then be content. Perhaps I just don't do that well enough."

"Whenever I have a plan I have to change it," said Rambril. "Circumstances intervene."

Dahl examined the lines on his hand closely, then held his palm at arm's length. "Now you see it, now you don't," he said, "You plan on the basis of what you see. The best plan comes from standing where you can see best."

"That changes too," replied Rambril. "In sunlight I can see Shar's garden from here. In the mist I may have to be no more than a spade handle's length away."

Dahl was still definite. "Planning," was what he said again.

Rambril confronted him. He spoke quietly and deliberately. "Perhaps grey people make grey plans."

Dahl shifted. "This is only what I think. I think other things too."

"Well," said Rambril, "if it is only what you think, it is not important. Drop it."

He went down the hill alone to see Shar.

"Hello," they both said. First the shyness, the carefulness.

"A grey morning," said Rambril.

"Don't mind my being grey also," Shar replied, and she pattered to and fro, touching, dusting, straightening.

Outside the mist was engulfing the morning. It moved in, swirling, then settled, suspended and damp. The garden was more than a spade handle's length away.

Shar did not listen to pop music on the radio when she was grey in the morning. She was grey but her face sustained its watchfulness.

Rambril puzzled over grey but watchful eyes as he carried the heavy things for her. "If you let the greyness enter you, what happens?" he thought. "Surely one must have walls, protection?"

"Over there." Shar pointed, cool, masterful in little things. Rambril watched the mist creep silently through the window and cling to chairs, curtains, bookshelves. Shar did not treat a house as a static thing, but changed it often. Soon the re-ordering was completed.

Rambril played the flute on the verandah. The sun was far-off, small, burning through coils of mist like the eye of a snake. Rambril spoke to it with his flute, to tell it of tenderness. His were not words of command. Perhaps the sun listened. As he wiped his flute to put it away the mist became tattered, the sun lit upon patches of grass, and upon the bold stand of sunflowers in Shar's garden.

Shar came and said, "Thank you. That was nice." And she said, "I have to go. I have to be at work." She was a nurse.

She dressed and made tea. Rambril remained on the verandah, reading from the notebook Shar had left lying there. "I minister to the sick, but I do not save them from themselves. If they would only be well for

186

themselves, they would never need be sick again. Ever."

"So it goes," he thought. "The fountain of well-being is inexhaustible."

They drank tea. Rambril said, "Sometimes well-being is lost in the mist. Do we sing to it, or command it to come?"

"Wrong question," said Shar. "Perhaps it sings to you, or commands you."

Rambril laughed. "Voices in the mist saying 'Don't worry. Be happy.'"

"I know," said Shar. "Sometimes the hard things press closely. Often they do quite well at ruling our consciousness. But isn't that the task, the first task? To not let the bad times rule our consciousness? We must save that first. The body will follow."

"And do you do that?" asked Rambril of the greyness that lingered.

"It is time for me to go," said Shar, standing.

Rambril walked back. He came upon Betty. "How is Dahl?" he asked.

"Okay," said Betty, flatly.

"Alright," said Rambril. "Wrong question. I'm sorry. How are you?"

"Okay," said Betty again.

They sat awhile, sun shining, uninterrupted, not even children to chatter or squawk. Such precious time.

"I think," said Rambril, "that things are not the way I thought they were."

"I can accept that," replied Betty. "What do you mean?"

"I would have thought it reasonable to say that I was lonely. And conversely, it would be unreasonable of you to say that you were lonely. You have your husband, your children. How could you be lonely? But sometimes, I think that you are, despite all appearances."

187

Betty made profound shifts of stance. Not shifts that manifested themselves openly. However, Rambril had touched her, regardless of what response she might make.

Betty sat very still. He puzzled, was this a response that indicated a quality of womanhood? Stillness might mean anything. It put him on the spot. He wondered, what would one do if one were master of the situation?

Fortunately Rambril was attentive enough to the needs of situations to act correctly. He reached out, and touched. Betty was tense. So Rambril said, although it did not come from him, "It is not I. It is the situation."

His arm around her, he felt her fear give way, and sadness unwind. He felt the fear of risk flee, for that moment. Betty allowed herself to receive comfort. And what Rambril gave, he gave without strings or expectation. For him this was no refuge, and there was no refuge to return to. It was simply the situation.

This scant comfort threatened them both. "So," Betty thought, "loneliness is toppled, but we must question everything now. We are all melting together. Rambril, Betty, Dahl. It is all food for the cooking pot."

Betty remembered. "You have been to see Shar?"

"Yes," replied Rambril. "I have."

"Well obviously," said Betty, "I want to know more."

"Yes, yes," said Rambril. "We talked. It was a grey morning. I guess I learned once again, from her, that one doesn't have to give in to grey mornings. One passes through them, like mist through a house. What time gives, one accepts."

Betty pondered. "Sometimes with Dahl, when the bad times come, I get angry, or I get sad, or

188

occasionally I get panicky. Because, it seems, the bad times don't just come; we have made them. Sometimes I think we will kill ourselves with the bad times."

Rambril met her eyes. Betty bowed her head, and Rambril rested his hands on her shoulders. "Whenever one wakes up, one has already been here a long time. And the scars and distortions are written into our bodies. In our eyes there are imprints, in our muscles there is tension.

"But let us say you are now awake. The sun is still shining, and finally you see that it can warm you. You open to it. This is how it should be. You find yourself feeling better, even the past is being remoulded. Scars fail to be painful."

"Perhaps you are right," said Betty. "Sometimes I see the sun. Other days it is just all grey. And then the gloom takes over."

"No, no, no," said Rambril gently, caressing her shoulder.

Dahl arrived, looking for Betty. There were plans in his head, for which her presence was necessary. "Let's go now," he said.

Rambril wandered alone among the trees, admiring their growth, and wondering why a branch should thrust itself out at just the point where it did. He made his eyes see the textures and the different shades of green, how each was itself, and how the whole was pleasing. Another day.

It is only such things as trees and rocks that are complete. People and people situations never are. Rambril said to Dahl, "I am not going to see Shar again. Shar doesn't have visitors, she only has intruders."

"You don't want to talk like that," replied Dahl.

"I would rather talk to trees," said Rambril.

"What has happened?" asked Dahl.

"Just conversations," said Rambril. "There are only two things in life: what people say, and what they do. Shar may talk, but she lives behind walls. The gates are made of iron."

"Okay," said Dahl. "And trees wear armour too. It prevents damage." Dahl had compassion for victims of war.

"There is no war. There is no threat," said Rambril, dispirited.

"No war, no threat. The truth is, there's no hope," replied Dahl, in the spirit of the moment.

"There's what is," answered Rambril. "Out of all that, I choose to talk to trees."

"There are two things in life," offered Dahl. "I am speaking about people. There is what is, and there is what they see. This is what makes us discontent. It is not necessarily unhealthy."

"Trees aren't discontent. They obey the elements – the sun, the soil, the rain and the wind. I would rather talk to trees."

"Well," said Dahl, "I am on my way to Shar's. I have to move some logs for her. Will you help me? You can talk to some dead trees."

"Okay," said Rambril, amused.

Shar and Betty were sitting on the verandah together, with the children playing a short distance away.

"Good morning," said Dahl, "and how is the sisterhood?"

"Close," replied Betty.

"That's worth a thought," said Dahl. "Alright, where are these logs?"

Rambril stood off to one side, practising tree-like silence.

Dahl and Shar discussed logs, their length, their diameter, where they were to go, and how close they were to be. Betty was busy wiping the children's noses, so Rambril's silence went unnoticed.

Off they went to move logs. They were heavy, of course, and demanded effort, demanded, in fact, copious perspiration. It was good. Push, roll, then nudge them into place. No talk, or just work-talk, children chatter in the distance, the sisterhood visible on the verandah. Rambril was enshrouded in mists of his own making. Push, roll, shuffle, shuffle, a break for breath. A good morning.

Shar had tea ready when they returned.

"Thank you," she said.

"Must go," said Rambril. "Things to do at home."

"Strange fellow," said Dahl to the sisterhood. "He doesn't talk much. Most of the time, I don't know what he's thinking."

"You spent the morning moving logs," replied Shar. "When you don't know what people are thinking, you look at what they do."

"Mmm," said Dahl. "I've heard it before, Thoughts are just thoughts. Who have you been talking to?"

"Trees," said Shar. They both laughed, for different reasons. Betty was smiling too. Betty and Dahl left hand in hand, children wrapped around them and running before them, leaving Shar to tidy her house and tend the garden.

What does one think? Nothing. What does one do? What is necessary. What happens? What was always going to happen. Who is responsible? Everyone, but those who know they are responsible are more responsible. So it goes.

How else will it be but unfinished? It is always still becoming – crisis, dearth, mystery and fulfilment.

Rambril wandered home and found things that needed doing. It took no desire: he did them. Doing what was necessary was sometimes like creating little children who said, "Thank you". Nice.

Rambril went and played in the garden for a while, pulling out weeds, shovelling manure, transplanting seedlings and praising the hollyhocks on their beauty. To the jasmine, showered with myriad star flowers, he offered his congratulations for its emergence after three years in the ground.

The hollyhocks giggled to one another like so many blushing children. "There goes Rambril. He loves us."

Betty arrived. "Excuse the hollyhocks," said Rambril. "They're only young."

"They're lovely."

"They're very generous. Youthful enthusiasm," laughed Rambril. He hugged Betty. She looked like she needed it. "What's the matter?" he asked.

"Dahl," she said, unsteadily. "Another fight."

"The anti-warrior?" said Rambril, "Still fighting?" He shrugged. "Obviously, this is what some people do," he thought.

"May I stay with you?" asked Betty.

"Where are the children?"

"Asleep in the car."

"Well, you have bright children. They know now to sleep through crises."

"I suppose so."

Rambril picked up one of the children to carry.

"I won't stay if you don't want."

"Where are you going to go?"

Betty scrambled for an answer.

"Stay," said Rambril, and carried the child inside.

Afterwards, they sat by the night fire, and Rambril asked her, "What are you going to do?" But Betty was not ready to answer.

"What has been happening? I thought things were going nicely with you two," he said.

Betty's voice was now steady. "In some ways, yes, but in other ways, no. I'm not good at digging up reasons. I was just starting to feel like another victim of war."

"War is over if you want it," quoted Rambril.

"Sounds good," said Betty drily. "Put it on a poster."

Rambril made more tea. They were both pensive. It was the situation. "I find that I am about three different people," he said musingly, as the fire encouraged. "I am Rambril-of-the-morning, Rambril-of-the-afternoon, and Rambril-of-the-evening. Each has his own set of rules. Once I learn how to get each of them to act appropriately and live together, I'll be alright."

Betty nodded. "I'm worst in the morning. Dahl is worst in the afternoon. But sometimes he carries on into the night. It's starting to affect the children."

Rambril finished his tea. He started off for bed. Betty was tired too.

That went on for a week: talk, sleep, look after the children, settle their squabbles, quiet their fears.

Where was Dahl? Rambril went to see.

"What the hell's going on?" snapped Dahl, from twenty paces. He didn't know what was going on, it was just his way of saying "Good morning" when he didn't feel good.

"Where is Betty?" asked Rambril evenly. He wondered what the answer would be.

"Cleared out," replied Dahl, "with the children. What the hell is going on?"

"Maybe she needed a rest from the war."

"What war? There's no war," Dahl snapped again, at closer range.

"Ho ho," replied Rambril, "and ho hum. Even I can smell a war. Especially at close range."

"I'm against war. I want peace."

"Peace is not something you can fight for, by definition."

"I just want peace."

"And excitement?" Rambril grinned, cheekily. Dahl threw a punch before he realised the essential contradiction. But Rambril was adept at ducking contradictions, and remained unscathed.

Dahl proceeded to be sullen. Rambril set about preparing a meal for them both. Dahl confessed hunger by his eagerness in consuming it. Rambril ate soberly, watching Dahl.

Dahl finished, left his plate and sat down in the sunlight, as withdrawn as a convalescent. Rambril did not speak, but tidied the kitchen and waited.

Dahl spoke. "What shall I do?"

"What are you prepared to do?"

"What can I do?"

"Fight, or accept."

"Well obviously, you've been telling me not to fight. So what choice does that leave me?"

"There's never a choice. You should do what you should do. Are you going to fight?"

"Oddly enough, no."

"Perhaps you will make the world suffer instead."

"No," said Dahl, suddenly clear. "I don't want to add to what's already there."

"That's good," said Rambril. He touched Dahl, shared his warmth, let it acknowledge the moment of clarity, that the moment might not be cold and lonely. Then he left.

When he returned to Betty he said, "You can do whatever you like."

"Not today," said Betty. "I'll go, but not today."

"As you wish."

Betty sat in the garden, and was enchanted by the blooms; they might have been conscious of her, humble maids with fragrant offerings. She wept, and let the tears fall. But she was glad Rambril did not see. The voice speaking to her was a stern mother's voice: "Some standards have to be maintained. Tears are not a release; they are a trap. Be strong. Your children need you to be strong. Don't cry, and if you must, hide your tears."

Betty always lost such arguments. The solid things around her became solid again. The colours leached from the flowers; the garden appeared dowdy.

Rambril saw it, but he was not a fighter. He helped cook the tea, and put the children to bed, and lit the fire for Betty. Then he slipped out.

He walked. He felt very still and very much in darkness. The night was like himself. So he thought, "And this too will pass." There was no point in walking, but no point in stopping, and no point in returning.

Eventually he arrived back and crept to bed, as hollow as a burnt-out log. The night turned to charcoal and froze over.

He woke before the dawn had come, out of featureless sleep, because one of the children was crying. He listened in the dark, and Betty's gentle footfalls crossed the room. Then he heard her singing, very softly, until the child forgot his sadness and snuggled down into the comfort Betty spun around him.

Rambril lay listening long after, while the silence hung about the house like wind-chimes waiting for the wind. "There are other songs to be sung," he thought. Morning. All the same ingredients: freshly brilliant sun, chatter of children, an early chill, soon surpassed by the day's heat. Birds on the roof, singing with religious devotion.

Betty packed, ready to go. Making talk, about ordinary things, as if this were all just the usual thing.

Rambril found himself in the same trap, feigning indifference. "It's just as well," he said, as he waved them off. "I have work to do."

Betty stopped the car at the gate, and beckoned him across. "Thank you," she said. "Keep working. Your place is looking nice. It was good to come here."

"I hope it works out," said Rambril.

"Perhaps it will, perhaps it won't. I'll try, but at least I know that whatever happens, I'll be okay. Thanks for that."

Rambril walked back slowly, seeing the weeds in his garden and plucking them out. "Why is it that I teach people things that I haven't seen myself?" But he was arrested by the need to say thank you.

Rambril went to visit Shar. She said, "How is Rambril-of-the-morning?"

"Ah, the sisterhood," he smiled. They sat on the verandah, and he said, "Just talk. Tell me what you think again. I am forgetting."

"What happened with Betty?" she asked. "Dahl has been driving me mad all week."

"How do you mean?"

"I think it's called ranting and raving. I don't like it. The quieter it is for me, the better."

"Some people would call your silence unhealthy, Shar. I think Dahl lives in his raging. He might not be happy, but he's full with living."

Shar shook her head. "Dahl has merely acquired bad living habits. Left to himself he'll do it until he dies, and bring his children up the same way."

"Oh, I agree. I just thought I'd say something in his defence. He's always too involved in the fighting to worry about defending himself."

"I'm sure he'll survive. What happened with Betty? You look well fed. Did she cook for you?"

"No, silly. I did most of the cooking. We had a lot of lentil curries."

Shar laughed. "Not every night, surely?"

"No, just a few. I made one that was quite hot, and it made Betty talk about Asia."

"People get nostalgic when they're going through crises."

Talk is creation. Two can do it, by following the thought in turn. Rambril followed. "But every crisis has its beginning. People always roll the film back to look for that beginning. Nostalgia is just a trap along the way."

"And was Betty nostalgic?"

Rambril was looking down on the garden. Always there were flowers. When one sort had fallen, another was opening out with its different colours, its own face, scent and exquisiteness. He nodded his praise to the roses.

"Yes, they're good, aren't they?" said Shar. "Will you have a cup of tea?"

When Rambril left Shar's house he climbed to the top of the hill, from where he could see down on her house, and where Betty and Dahl were trying out as partners again. Then his own house a little further off.

That was in the valley. Rolling like larger waves were the green backs of hills covered with trees, as they should be. Hills are modest creatures, and enjoy the rustle of leaves about their shoulders, and the sway of trunks on their crowns, like flags waving.

"Om," said Rambril. What else? He walked home. It was a silent, peaceful afternoon walk home, with the sun melting into the hills like butter over a gentle fire. "In the end we all surrender," he said to the sun. "It's alright." The sky glowed – the last smile of the day.

*   *   *   *   *

Yunwin

Yunwin was a fair child, but the daughter of two cruel parents. As far back as she could recall she remembered only the presence of arguing and grumbling, and of having to creep along sometimes under the weight of one parent or the other's brooding silences between the fights. Her father would grumble about his work, or about how poor he was, or he would scold his wife for not being a good cook, or for being careless, or anything else that came to mind.

In turn, her mother was sullen, or she would burst out suddenly in anger, cursing her husband's rudeness. Yunwin was treated little better than they treated each other; she was cursed as a burden, scorned for being clumsy, or stupid, or unhelpful. When still far too young for it, she was expected to help with the dishes, or sweep the house, or bring in the wood for the fire. She learned the caution of the wallaby, and ate her meals as if the dogs would be set at her heels at any moment.

One day, still full of the vulnerability of youth, Yunwin was told by her mother that she must go to the forest and find some mushrooms for dinner. "Take this basket with you, and mind that you come back with enough," she said, "otherwise it's precious little supper you'll be having, that's for sure."

Yunwin took the basket, trembling slightly. She had always been afraid of the forest. Seldom had she entered it, and the presence of her cruel-hearted father at those times had done little to still or tame her fears. She could not storm through the forest in the same violent manner that was his custom.

She took the basket, her throat stopped and swollen, her eyes brimmed with tears. She tried to remain steady, for she knew there was no possibility of her mother relenting. All Yunwin would get would be a further lashing with her mother's sharp-edged tongue, or a blow across her back with the nearest stick.

But when her mother had marched off, telling her not to waste her time picking flowers, she let the tears fall, no longer able to hold them back. But knowing she could not stay where she was, in sight of the house, she grabbed the basket and plunged into the trees.

The grass gave way to bushes and undergrowth, and the shadow of the trees was all around her, spraying her with mottled light as she moved. Around her the plants seemed dangerously alive, slithering, rustling, lashing at her with every step. Sticks were snakes, every brush of a leaf was a spider, the dark shadows among bushes were larger threats, perhaps wild dogs, or even a rogue bull.

Yunwin tried to remember directions and landmarks. It was difficult to do that while her fears crowded her, but then as she kept on moving her fears seemed to fade a little with the realisation that she had come this far without being bitten, stung, bruised or broken.

Soon she was able to take some notice of important landmarks – a tree with a curious branch, a boulder shaped like a whale, a particular twist in the pathway. She was able to look around and take delight in the flowers that were blooming, and the butterflies that glided by. A pair of blue wrens accompanied her for a while, chattering in little songs to each other, darting from a branch in a bush to another just overhead in a tree.

Her basket began to fill with mushrooms, as her mother had requested. One here, a couple there, she found them on her way.

When Yunwin came back she glowed with the joy that the forest-life had showered upon her. The forest had taken her timid spirit and shown her the full reach, the soft touch, the grandeur and the beauty, of its own heart. Yunwin had found her first friend in the form of the forest itself.

Her mother did not fail to see the change in her daughter. Her reaction was immediate, and harsh. "You have wasted your day," she scolded, even though the basket was full of mushrooms. "I have been washing all day, and who has been there to help me? Not you, I see. Did it take you all day to collect this much?" she added scornfully.

Her tirade was long and bitter, and Yunwin stood in the brunt of it, too stunned with bewilderment to consider defending herself.

In her room alone that night she sat, silently and awake, long after the house-light had been quenched, and the stars alone twinkled above the blackness of tree-shapes. The thoughts came to her slowly but clearly.

"I love the trees," she thought. "I love the trees even when the light is as faint as tiny stars, and the trees are only shapes against their faintness. And if this is the only light then I still love. Mother, please allow me."

So Yunwin now knew, and the knowledge stayed with her, that there are other spirits in the world than of peevishness and cruelty. She was sent to the forest again, with none of her former trepidation. There, in the presence of the trees, and the other harmonious lives she now knew were there, she made this pledge:

"I will add no more to the cruelty that is already in the world. I will remember the spirits of loveliness and peace when I am surrounded by those who are cruel or thoughtless."

Night fell suddenly. Perhaps she stayed that long because of the comfortable place she had found that day, or because of being tired from crying, for her parents had both been particularly harsh to her that morning.

But there came with it no fear. The stars were clear enough to tempt her to count them. They twinkled in their familiar formations, faithful and quiet observers. Yunwin spread her arms abroad to receive the blessing they offered. She slept.

In the morning there seemed no reason to hurry back home. It was later in the day that her father found her and dragged her home, beating her as his annoyance swelled into periodic outbursts of anger. He hurled abuse at her all the way. She was ungrateful, stupid, a burden to her parents. She was lazy, thoughtless, irresponsible.

When they reached home her mother added her own bitter reproaches to all that her father had flung at her. She was sent to her room, and the door was locked. Yunwin was not frozen into despair by this treatment. She glowed with the remembering, the patterns of the stars in their time-old dance, the fibrous, elastic strength of grandfather trees, and the weaving elusiveness of butterflies. The butterflies most of all, because they had startled her at play, were so tiny and yet so magnificent.

It did not make any difference to her father. He beat her and forced her to spend her play-time working for him. Her mother was different. She sensed the change in Yunwin. But in her case that made it harder for Yunwin, for her mother was crueller than ever. Yunwin had not a moment's peace, from dawn until dusk, with running about from one job to another, and being abused because the jobs were not done well enough.

Night after night Yunwin lay, still with her remembering, but filled with increasing despair at her present, seemingly endless situation. She found that she was retreating to her room more often. What did she do there?

Very little she did, sitting on her bed and staring at the walls. "I can't do this forever," she thought. Then she tried to talk herself out of her feelings, but that was not what she needed either.

A day dawned when her mother simply did not want her around. Yunwin was called, and her mother had her basket in her hand. "Make yourself useful," she snapped. "Go to the forest and bring back a basket of mushrooms."

And Yunwin was off, running, with the basket in one hand. It was a gleeful release, and she could not hide it, although she knew that she would pay for it later.

Again the forest had its peculiar beauties to displace the gloom that usually surrounded her. Wonders that were always unexpected, tiny, or hard to reach, or cunningly hidden. She found them by the dozens, wanted to collect them all in her basket. It was enough to bathe her soul in such waters, and be content and happy.

She returned home late, and her mother began scolding her as soon as she entered. "Ungrateful child, never here when you're supposed to be! Wasting your days in selfish meanderings!"

Yunwin was struck by the sadness of it. The door slammed on her despair again. But her path had already been trodden. In the thick of the night, when the stars were distant and faint behind the finest curtain of mist, Yunwin rose without thinking and packed her bag. On tip-toe she crept through the silence of the house, and with a deep sigh at the gate she was on her way.

Her sigh was gathered and became one with the mist as it drenched the house and all around it, a film of tears for the morning sun to dissolve.

Yunwin travelled all night. She went deep into the forest, for a day and then another day. In that time she saw nobody. But on the next day she came upon a man.

He was in the middle of a clearing, singing in a strange, detached fashion and clapping his hands. He swayed backwards and forwards, and he obviously did not regard his audience as inhabiting the space immediately in front of him. Yunwin watched the singer, listening to the singing. The sun rose higher and the singer's continuity began to falter. He lapsed into prolonged silences. But still he did not rise.

Yunwin came forward. She watched the man at close quarters. Finally he looked up at her questioningly. "So vulnerable," she said. "Follow me."

And man followed. "Who are you?" she asked.

"Mu," he replied. But no more would he add.

Every day, it seemed, he would sing. The sun would train its eye upon him, and he would sit beneath it. The songs he sang were obviously songs to cross vast reaches of time or space, but mostly Yunwin couldn't understand them.

Just that they were necessary and good. Perhaps they were messages to angels, perhaps he was summoning up God Himself, or pleading for the intervention of some higher beings. But she accepted them. And when he had done she would guide them to a place to eat, or if they were very fortunate, even a bed for the night.

They wandered until Yunwin no longer knew how long it was that they had been wandering. Mu was her child, and her master. She led, and she followed.

But paths turn, and Yunwin knew it when it happened. The message came to return home. Yunwin did not afterwards recall how the message came. Was it a message delivered in her heart? Was it a piece of casual gossip from a passer-by? Mu could not remember either. They both trod their paths seeking what was before them, not questioning the landscape behind.

The house, when they saw it, had a stillness about it that Yunwin could not recall being there before. There were flowers in several corners, blossoming timidly but sweetly.

It was as if her father no longer trampled as much as he had done before, and the flowers had been ready, waiting and wanting to grace the yard.

Yunwin entered alone, not knowing what to expect. But as she closed the door she knew it was a death. Strange it was how the very air spelled it out.

It was a death, but it was not what she would have expected. She turned and walked back out to where Mu was waiting. Mu was silent. No song was filling the air, on its way to far-off destinations. He was not sitting in his customary detachment in the sun, pouring himself forth to the gods. His eyes were the utmost of calmness, and they embraced Yunwin wordlessly as she emerged from the cottage.

"Your father wishes to see you," he said quietly, and led her across to the far side of the clearing.

Her father was wandering about near the fresh grave. He saw her and his eyes flashed briefly. But there was not the outburst that would have taken place formerly. His manner was surly, but subdued. When he spoke it was a mere grumble, the fire of his usual anger now only an ember, and perhaps that only out of habit.

"So you've come back," he said. "You go away, your mother dies, and you come back."

Yunwin had no answer. She was still held by the sudden peace she had met. How was she to say that to her father? But her father did not pursue the conversation further. He wandered off towards the forest, axe over his shoulder.

Yunwin let him go. She was seeing the grave of her mother. She knelt down, and sat there a long time. She went and searched for a piece of wood, and wrote on it – "AT REST" – and put this at the grave's head, along with some flowers that she had gathered, the new ones she had seen, and others that she remembered.

Late in the day she returned, and Mu was there, waiting calmly.

"We will go," she said. "I would like to stay, but my father would be uncomfortable. There is too much that he would remember."

The scent of the day's flowers still freshened the breeze, still all new, still timid, but unblighted. The cottage in the clearing was cleansing itself of its years of aching, the hurt that had been Yunwin's, but her mother's too. Yes, and her father's.

"My father will be alright," she said to Mu, for she sensed his thought. "He won't fight with mother any more. Now perhaps, they can be together. In time," she added, "he may even stop fighting with me."

Mu nodded his head. Somehow it seemed that his purpose was no longer in singing, but he felt more alive than ever, and Yunwin was within the circle of love that radiated from him. Yunwin knelt by the grave again, and she wept, but she spoke quietly her last words to her mother.

"Once my tears were a river between us, but now they flow from the same place where you are now, and heal the world, in their small way."

No voice spoke, but it was Mu's thought that responded:

"Blessings upon this place."

In the evening, when Yunwin's father settled himself by the fire, the blessing hung in the air. He was surprised by new thoughts, and it seemed to him that there was much less to be irritable about than he used to think. Obstinate as he was, he would not let himself be wide open to joy, but he helped himself to a small bowl of the soup that Yunwin had left for him, and saved the rest for tomorrow.

*   *   *   *   *